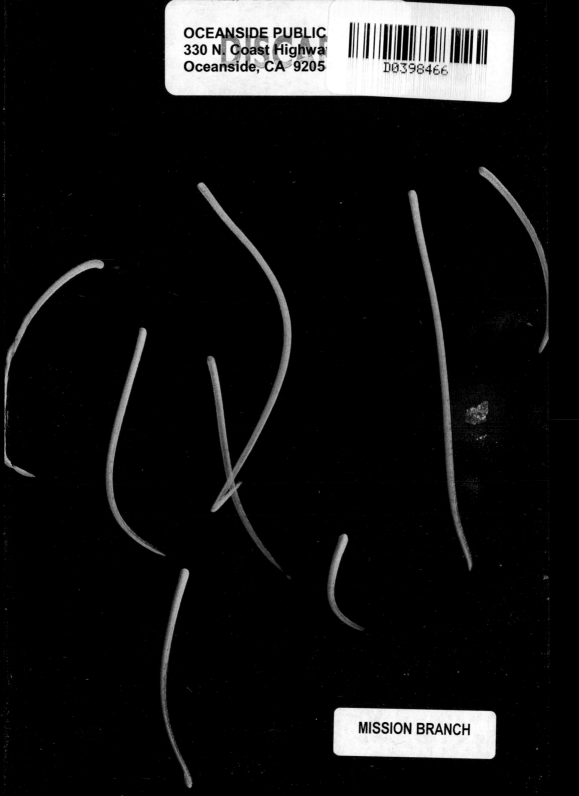

IN
MORTAL
DANGER

IN
MORTAL
DANGER

The Battle for America's Border and Security

TOM TANCREDO

WND BOOKS

AN IMPRINT OF CUMBERLAND HOUSE PUBLISHING, INC.

NASHVILLE, TENNESSEE

IN MORTAL DANGER
A WND BOOK
PUBLISHED BY CUMBERLAND HOUSE PUBLISHING, INC.
431 Harding Industrial Drive
Nashville, Tennessee 37211

Cover design by Linda Daly

Library of Congress Cataloging-in-Publication Data

Tancredo, Thomas G., 1945–
   In mortal danger : the battle for America's border and security / Tom Tancredo.
      p.   cm.
   Includes bibliographical references and index.
   ISBN-13: 978-1-58182-527-5 (hardcover : alk. paper)
   ISBN-10: 1-58182-527-7 (hardcover : alk. paper)
   1. Illegal aliens—United States. 2. United States—Emigration and immigration.
   3. United States—Emigration and immigration—Government policy. 4. Border patrols—United States. 5. Terrorism—United States—Prevention. 6. Assimilation (Sociology). 7. Mexico—Emigration and immigration. I. Title.
   JV6465.T36 2006
   364.1'3—dc22   2006012396

Printed in the United States of America

2 3 4 5 6 7 8 9 10—10 09 08 07 06

To

MADELEINE COSMAN,

a dedicated warrior in the battle against illegal aliens. Her vast
knowledge of the deleterious effects of the invasion now
under way and her brilliant manner of expressing them made
her loved by patriots everywhere and feared by the cult of
multiculturalism. Some of my fondest memories include
sharing the stage with her at immigration-reform events and
basking in the glow of her wit, wisdom, and courage.

CONTENTS

Preface   9

Part 1: The American Identity

1: What It Meant to Be an American   21

2: Destroying Our Roots   25

3: Imparting the Cult of Multiculturalism   37

4: Adopting Bilingualism   53

5: Clash of the Civilizations   65

6: The Barbarians Are Past the Gate   79

7: Autumn in Beslan   89

Part 2: Our Broken Immigration System

8: Our Porous Borders   101

9: The Myths of Immigration   111

10: System Breakdown   117

11: Politics of Immigration   127

12: Breach in Security   137

13: Mexico's Lawless Border   143

14: The Economics of Mass Migration   155

15: The Threat to Our Health System by Illegal Immigration   163

16: Environmental Impact from Illegal Immigration   173

Part 3: What Needs to Be Done

17: Steps for Reform   183

18: Preserving Our National Existence   191

Conclusion: Your Assignment   207

Notes   211

Index   219

PREFACE

This GUY's got an agenda!" my opponent screamed into the microphone as he pointed an accusatory finger at me.

Although this happened rather recently, the charge has been hurled at me in almost every political campaign I have ever waged—starting with my successful race for the Colorado legislature in 1975. Every time this happens, I answer the same way: "You bet your life I do!"

I have always wanted to advance the agenda of limited government and enhanced individual freedom. Although it sounds a bit audacious, I want to participate in the reintroduction in this country of the concept that America is a unique place, not just a place where we can reap the economic and political benefits afforded by the labors of those who lived before us. I want our borders to be secure and those who have violated them to be deprived of the benefits lawful citizens enjoy, lest the concept of citizenship be rendered meaningless. I want immigrants seeking that citizenship to assimilate and sever their ties to their countries of origin. And I want us to encourage—not discourage—that assimilation. Perhaps even more audaciously, I want to do what I can to defend the West in the clash of civilizations that threatens humanity with a return to the Dark Ages.

The parts of my agenda that have generated the most trouble for me deal with the security of our borders and with my criticism of what I refer to as the "cult of multiculturalism." Indeed, these are parts that I find most exhilarating, the parts about which I am most passionate. The battle to hold a diverse nation together by a common adherence to the American creed—which is most easily defined by our Constitution and our founders' Declaration of Independence as opposed to a creed exemplified by an almost religious devotion to diversity—seems worth the effort. Amazingly, these items on my agenda have put me at odds with my own party and President George W. Bush. You must understand, however, that I never imagined that these differences would be the chief hallmark of my tenure in Congress. I ran for office with the intent of being a team player. I assumed, naively, that my goals coincided with the party's and the president's. It hasn't worked out that way.

I have lived by my commitment to do everything I can to avoid falling into the political pitfall that happens to so many congressman after a few years in office: simply taking up space. To my surprise, perhaps the phrase "lightning rod" is used more often than any other to describe me. Although writers or speakers in a negative connotation primarily use it, the description suits me fine.

Sometimes it has seemed to me as if far too many folks seeking elective office do so primarily because they want to be *in the office*. Once they decide which office they want, they then construct the belief system and rhetoric they believe they need to get it. Once elected, they spend the rest of their time figuring out what they have to do, say, and think in order to keep it. I have served with folks who knew they could not be elected in certain districts unless they changed parties. They did so without a second thought. After all, the goal was the office, not the furthering of a cause or an agenda. Needless to say, it is wise for citizens to steer clear of these folks and refuse to reward them with their votes.

Admittedly, discerning every candidate's motivation for running for office requires some study and reflection. It's worth the effort, and it's better than relying on name recognition, physical appearance, or even party affiliation. When all else fails, look for passion.

I have learned that one cannot rely on party affiliation alone to determine the authenticity of a candidate. This is often brought home to me during discussions in the Congress of issues such as immigration. That's because members of both parties work together to advance selfish goals on behalf of special-interest groups and businesses while at the same time ignoring the danger and damage that the sheer volume of immigration—legal and otherwise—is doing to America. And make no mistake about it: the pursuit of these selfish goals is causing permanent, long-term damage to our country. Eventually, our culture will reach a point of no return. I have no choice but to raise my voice as loudly as I can, even if that means criticizing my own party.

There is a price to pay for standing up for what I believe rather than just going along with my party. My differences of opinion with my Republican colleagues and my willingness to voice them publicly mean that I almost certainly will never be the chairman of a major House committee. After President Bush's most trusted political adviser, Karl Rove, told me to "never darken the doorsteps of the White House" because of my criticism of the president, I expected no calls to confer with him on any immigration issues. If ever Congress does pass immigration-reform legislation, my name won't be on it as a principal sponsor. During a debate recently with one of my Republican colleagues over the issue, he said I should resign from the party because my views were not the same as his or the president's.

I get little or no support from business political-action committees (PACs), largely because many businesses and corporations depend on cheap illegal-immigrant labor to hold down their costs and increase their profits, thus denying better-paying jobs to American workers. In fact, one corporation in my congressional district, First Data Corporation, even formed a PAC to ensure my defeat, telling a county commissioner in my district that if I didn't "shut up on the immigration issue," they might move the company out of the county. Ironically, First Data owns Western Union, a company that makes millions of dollars annually from facilitating the transfer of funds from foreign nationals living in the United States to families back home.

Former House majority leader Tom DeLay (R-TX) once called me into his office to tell me I had "no career" in Congress. He was pretty specific about the possible problems I could face if didn't change my tactics.

I understand the need for party discipline, and I don't blame the leadership for reacting to my outspoken criticism. I have, however, always thought of myself as a loyal Republican, and as such, I'll do what I can to push the party toward a closer connection to its basic principles. There are signs that the party is getting the message, not just from me, but also from the grass roots. The House passage of a strong immigration-enforcement bill in December 2005 is just one indicator that the ship of state may finally be turning. Whether or not it will do so quickly enough to avoid a disaster at the polls remains to be seen.

So with or without the blessing of my party or the president, and for as long as I have a forum, I will continue to raise my voice and use my vote in Congress. I will continue to rail against the permissive attitudes regarding immigration enforcement held by most of my colleagues and the president. I will always challenge their adherence to the idea that borders are anachronistic barriers to the free flow of goods, services, *and* people. We in government are collectively not doing enough to protect America from a range of threats that are working against us, and we seem oblivious to the fact that these threats place us in mortal danger.

Believe me, like most people, I want to be liked and accepted by my colleagues. Being called "Mr. Chairman" would be a heady trip. I would enjoy being invited to the White House for informal chats about policy. But I have long since given up on such aspirations and take solace in the fact that, every other January, I take an oath of office that does not include a vow of loyalty to my party or the president. That vow, instead, is to uphold and defend the Constitution of the United States. I do the best I can to be faithful to that vow. But all I have to advance this agenda are a voice and a vote. I pledge to use each as effectively as I can. I will do all I can do and put the rest in God's hands.

The topics covered in this book are related to and part of the great immigration-policy debate that has consumed much of my public life over the past decade, but they also transcend that debate in fundamental ways. I write about our porous borders and our broken immigration system, but they are only symptoms of deeper problems in our culture and our politics.

I begin with the most fundamental question of all, what it means to be an American, and then I examine the forces and ideas that are working to undermine our loyalties and our institutions. It goes much deeper than open borders and massive illegal immigration, much deeper than the costs of providing services to fifteen to twenty million illegal ("undocumented") aliens. The television images of thousands of people scrambling across the border at night pose a striking image, but that picture does not explain what is happening within our culture and our society.

What is happening on our borders is one story, but what is happening within America is an even more disturbing tale. The relationship between our immigration policies and our future as a functioning cultural entity needs to be understood by the Minutemen and all the partisans who have been engaged in the struggle to achieve secure borders.

In these opening chapters on culture, values, loyalties, and the roots of the American identity, I try to explore the ramifications of these deeper problems. America is facing an "identity crisis," a crisis not caused by massive immigration but certainly exacerbated by it. We need to understand the underlying causes and issues, not just the surface manifestations of the crisis.

Chapter 4's description of the Denver Public Library's adoption of bilingualism is a good example of probing an issue to its core and asking basic questions that were either ignored or covered up by the leaders of the institutions involved. The public library's move to bilingualism is a major development in our civic culture and one that might have escaped public scrutiny had I not sounded an alarm. The debate over that engineered policy change involved all the basic questions of national identity. The desire of Denver politicians to obfuscate the issue and avoid a public debate is symptomatic of how difficult it is to confront these issues constructively and productively in the present age of political correctness. Under the guise of "providing better services to new immigrants," the Denver Public Library is now promoting and underwriting the balkanization of our community. All of the key issues in this cultural battle were enjoined in this case—bilingualism, the proper use of taxpayer funds, "Sanctuary City" immigration policies, and the lack of accountability of public officials. The citizens of Denver lost that battle, but the nation can learn from that experience.

The several chapters on our broken immigration system explain the many facets of a problem that has been at center stage for the past year. I delve into the economics of massive immigration, the devastating impact on our communities, the national security threats, the strain on our health-care system, and the consequences for our environment and quality of life. I also offer some concrete suggestions for reforms that might slow down or possibly reverse our slide into social chaos.

I do not relish the personal attacks and occasional ridicule thrown at me as a result of my "agitation" on these issues. I may have become a "lightning rod" for some of these contentious issues, but I must remind my critics of one thing: a lightning rod is a silent sentinel until there is lightning. I did not create the lightning. It is being created instead by the dangerous and myopic policies that generate outrage among decent American citizens of all ethnic backgrounds.

We are living in times of great cultural and political turmoil. While radical Islamists are killing Americans in Iraq and plotting apocalyptic acts of terror for our homeland, we are wrestling with the question Sam Huntington poses in the title of his brilliant book *Who Are We?*

The question of who we are is not a question to be examined and pondered only by academics and cultural gadflies. The question is brought into sharp relief by the rhetoric and demands voiced by the speakers and sponsors in the mass demonstrations of March and April 2006. An estimated two million protesters marched in more than fifty cities on April 10, from Los Angeles to Atlanta, from Phoenix to Chicago. The protesters were demanding a blanket amnesty for current illegal aliens under the banner of "immigrant rights," but they were also demanding much more.

The organizers of these mass demonstrations have an agenda that surpasses mere amnesty for twelve to fifteen million illegal aliens, and that agenda is clearly visible in the placards and banners carried by many of the marchers. After the public backlash caused by the prominence of Mexican flags at the first demonstrations on March 25, organizers in April handed out American flags and discouraged Mexican flags, but the rhetoric hardly changed. The underlying theme of the protests was, "We are here, we are not going home, we demand the right to cross your borders anytime we choose, and we demand our human rights."

The mainstream popular media, as usual, accepted the radical rhetoric and called these events "immigrant-rights protests." Yet the truth is that "immigrants" already have rights protected by the courts. What the organizers are demanding is that the rights now afforded *legal* immigrants also be awarded to *illegal* aliens. Any suggestion that any sane immigration policy must begin with secure borders is dismissed as "racist."

The sheer size of the protests is indeed awesome, but that size should not be so surprising when viewed as the fruit of the combined effort of a hundred national organizations: the Catholic Church and dozens of other religious bodies; the Service Employees International Union; the large network of Spanish-language radio and television stations and newspapers; large national radical Hispanic groups like

LULAC and the National Council of La Raza; and local school districts that allowed—and in some cases actually encouraged—students to participate. Many Far-Left organizations have also joined in promoting the protests, such as the ANSWER Coalition (Act Now to Stop War and End Racism), and the avowedly communist Workers World Party. In Los Angeles, a cochairman of the April 10 march, Juan Jose Gutierrez of the Marxist-dominated Latino Movement USA, announced, "This is the beginning of a movement that is going to call for a national work stoppage."[1]

Viewed from a different perspective, we can say that 2 million people marched in protest on April 10, and 297 million Americans did not join them. Yet, unfortunately, some members of Congress are easily spooked by the threat of a massive Hispanic voting bloc, despite evidence from recent elections that Hispanics vote as individuals, not as puppets dancing to the tune of radical college professors proclaiming the rebirth of "Aztlan."

Meanwhile, the principal of a high school in Longmont, Colorado, has banned the display of the U.S. (or any other) flag because he says such displays can be "disruptive." And in a suburban middle school just north of Denver, a student was threatened with disciplinary measures for wearing blue jeans, a white shirt, and a red sweater. Apparently the color combination was too suggestive of the flag!

Our ability to weather this storm will surely determine how long, or even if, the United States will survive as a unique nation-state. The threats to our future are external (Islamofascism) and internal (the cult of multiculturalism). Together they form such a potent adversary that I believe we are—as much as any time in our history—in mortal danger.

I want to express my appreciation to Charles Heatherly, Hugh Fowler, and Jason Miller for their priceless contributions to this book. And I want to especially thank Jon E. Dougherty for his suggestions and review of the text.

IN
MORTAL
DANGER

PART 1

The American Identity

1

What It Meant to Be an American

A nation, as a society, forms a moral person, and every member of it is personally responsible for his society.

—Thomas Jefferson

WHEN OUR FOREFATHERS SETTLED the original thirteen colonies, they were driven by a passionate resolve to provide the best possible lives for their families, to freely practice their religion, to build wealth through farming and industrial opportunities, and most important, to govern themselves. But their dreams of "life, liberty, and the pursuit of happiness" were not easily achieved. When England began raising taxes and issuing punitive edicts—such as closing the port of Boston—the American colonists banded together to revolt and to govern themselves. A nation was born.

Today, many still look to America as they hope for freedom and prosperity. They cross its borders to settle their families, much like the original settlers did more than three hundred years ago. Yet while more than one million immigrants annually choose to settle in this country legally, millions more pour over the borders illegally. While most illegal immigrants come to America for the same reasons the early colonists did, ironically they reap the benefits of a fractured system that leaves them unaccountable and indifferent to what it means to be an American. When these aliens begin their American experience by breaking the law and then realize that act has no significant consequences, it is hard to convince them—or anyone else—that the nation is committed to the rule of law.

Of course the America to which all immigrants flock today is quite different from the one to which immigrants of previous generations came.

In America in the 1950s, the term "civic duty" had the connotation of selfless devotion to the American creed. Students once learned of the hardships endured by patriotic volunteer soldiers who made sacrifices for the ideas and ideals embodied in the documents that (because so many were illiterate) were read to them by their officers at Valley Forge. In America in the 1950s, people of faith were regarded as the pillars of their community, and it was perfectly acceptable to display an American flag on your house.

Today, however, our schools and almost every other social institution in our society send a totally different message. Civic duty, for instance, is currently considered by far too many office holders as an obligation to erase any vestige of pride in the symbols or the substance of the land of the free and home of the brave.

When my grandparents came to this country, they had two choices: they either worked or they starved. That was it. There was nothing else. There was no such thing as a welfare program. This meant that certain things became very important—like learning English. Knowing the language was necessary to work your way out of poverty and to begin to climb the ladder leading to the American dream. Of course, my grandparents, like most of their peers, *wanted* to cut the ties that bound them to the old country and to connect with their new land. At that time, this desire and the economic forces at play combined to encourage the assimilation of immigrants. At that time, assimilation was made easier by the fact that most immigrants came from faraway places, and opportunities to maintain a political or emotional attachment to those faraway places was difficult.

In today's America, immigrants are welcomed by a society intoxicated with the idea of multiculturalism. Today's immigrants quickly become aware that there is no need to leave their old language or various attachments behind because the only cause they will be required to espouse is allegiance to the ideology of radical multiculturalism.

Some say we have morphed into a society so soft and self-centered that we cannot prosper like those who came before us without the labors of an army of serfs in our fields and factories.

At one time, employers were concerned that their workers did not have criminal backgrounds. They wanted people of good moral character who had a good work ethic. Today they prefer lawbreakers. Their excuse is parroted in any discussion of illegal immigration: they take the jobs that Americans will not do. But that is nonsense. I don't buy it. In most instances, that statement should end with, "for the amount I am able to pay illegal workers." I worked those same jobs when I was young, as did my children. More important, as laborious as they can be, those jobs taught me what it meant to work and earn a dollar. Today, because of the flood of illegal workers who are willing to work cheaply, the rate of unemployment among our teenagers is the highest it has ever been.

I don't know if we have become a nation of the same kind of self-indulgent hedonists that characterized the failed societies of past civilizations, but I do know that there is much here worth saving. To do that we must not only look at what it means to *be* American, but we also must notice how *becoming* an American has changed over the years.

Every two weeks there are services for those who are being sworn in as new American citizens. Every time I attend such a service, I tell these new citizens two things: (1) Welcome to the United States, and (2) Thank you for doing it the right way. Every time we give an illegal immigrant the same benefits available to these new citizens who have obeyed the law, we mock the naturalization process. It is an insult to everyone who has taken the time and expended the energy to go through the process of becoming an American citizen.

Today, citizenship has been devalued because our government allows foreigners to live here illegally and provides them with the same benefits as citizens. In a recent op-ed piece, Peggy Noonan asked, "What does it mean that your first act on entering a country is breaking its laws?" Oh, how times have changed! She points out eloquently how, in just two generations, becoming an American has changed from being a prize to an entitlement:

23

Here is what is true of my immigrants and of the immigrants of America's past: They fought for citizenship. They earned it. They waited in line. They passed the tests. They had to get permission to come. They got money that was hard earned and bought a ticket. They had to get through Ellis Island or the port of Boston or Philadelphia, get questioned and eyeballed by a bureaucrat with a badge, and get the nod to take their first step on American soil. . . .

They knew citizenship was not something cheaply held but something bestowed by a great nation. . . .

Did the fact that they had to earn it make joining America even more precious?

Yes. Of course.[1]

The battle for our way of life must continue beyond the halls of Congress and into the streets. We must talk about the value of Western civilization and the principles it embodies. We must begin to explore them passionately, perhaps in a way that has not happened in this country for almost a century. After all, if we just live in America with no particular philosophy, no set of ideas or ideals that are worth our allegiance, then the opponents of Western civilization will continue to corrupt our children's minds with false ideas.

The terrorists who seek to kill us know exactly who they are. They have no identity crisis. They know and believe with all their being the philosophy and religious underpinnings of their worldview. They are intent upon spreading it with word and deed, by violence if necessary.

Consequently, when we fail to tell our children and newcomers to America about our history and ideals, we are telling them that there is nothing of value, nothing worth their sacrifice. When we fail to pass on the ideals that make our nation what it is and imply that all cultures are the same, that all values are relative, we are sowing the seeds of our own demise.

Instead, we must use our schools, churches, and government to reestablish a connection with and allegiance to the principles of Western civilization. Those principles are embodied in the Judeo-Christian ethic, and whether we follow them or not will surely determine the fate of the nation.

2

Destroying Our Roots

Great nations, no matter how ethnically diverse, have a common bond that unites its people. . . . That common bond is language.

—Dennis Gallagher, New York City Councilman

I'VE LIVED IN AND around the wonderful city of Denver all my life. Part of its rich cultural history is that it was the first city in the nation to have a Columbus Day parade. In fact, Colorado was the first state to observe Columbus Day as a state-sanctioned holiday. In 2005 we marked the one hundredth anniversary of that recognition.

Because this part of our history infuriates the cult of multicultural-ism, the general understanding of who Christopher Columbus was is under constant assault. The authors of a ninth-grade history book once used by a charter school in my district declared, "Columbus discovered America and destroyed paradise." The life and character of the man who introduced Europe to the American continent faces an ongoing "decon-struction." The goal of the radicals is to ban Columbus Day observances. This is just another example of the all-out war the intolerant (under the guise of toleration) are waging on Western civilization itself.

With the goal of trying to force Denver to become the first city that *ends* Columbus Day celebrations, the American Indian Movement (AIM) and other groups since the early 1990s have annually protested the observance, sometimes using more than signs and shouts to get their message out. They have gone to court, relentlessly pressured city officials into revoking the parade organizers' licenses, and staged violent and radical protests to disrupt the observance.

The groups trying to wipe out Columbus Day celebrations in Denver, without question, represent a minority of the city's residents, but nonetheless, the city's leaders have been largely sympathetic to them. In fact, between 1992—the five-hundredth anniversary of Columbus's discovery of the New World—and 2000, the city didn't have a parade commemorating this historic discovery. In 2005, Denver mayor John Hickenlooper—professing to be "sick and tired" of the flap between the Indian activists and the city's ethnic Italian population—proposed replacing the Columbus Day parade with a generic Italian heritage festival.[1]

Before this happened, I had never actually participated in the Denver Columbus Day parade. But after AIM and its supporters began their ridiculous and politically motivated attacks on Columbus himself—depicting him as an evil man who came to America to "destroy paradise," commit atrocities, and perpetrate genocide against the native tribes—I decided to participate, something I have continued to do every year since then.

In my first year, parade organizers wanted me to ride on the back of a flatbed truck. But shortly before the parade began, police officers asked if I were aware of the number of death threats that had been made against me. Half-jokingly, I answered, "Well, any more than *usual*?" One officer deadpanned in reply, "Oh yeah," then proceeded to tell me about the evidence they had collected along the parade route to substantiate the veracity of the threats. Later I was told the police had found bullets taped to the inside of a trash barrel along the route. The flatbed truck idea was out, and I walked the parade route with officers flanking me for a degree of protection.

My first parade appearance went off without much of a hitch, but on several occasions since then, protesters have broken through barricades and rushed some participants, creating damage and causing police to arrest hundreds of people. Some Indian protesters have thrown red paint in the streets to symbolize blood; others have lain down in the streets to block traffic; still others remained on the sidelines, beating drums and blowing smoke toward the crowds. Eventually the protests became severe enough that the city council adopted new laws prohibiting anyone from blocking parade routes.[2]

But the insanity over Columbus Day isn't confined to Denver. In 2005, Berkeley, California, became the first city in the nation to replace Columbus Day with an observance and celebration of "Indigenous People's Day." This event focuses primarily on Indians. All of this, of course, comes at the expense of Western culture and civilization.[3] "I'm sure there's some people that prefer to celebrate Columbus Day," said Berkeley "councilmember" Max Anderson, "but generally I think [Indigenous People's Day] is broadly supported."[4]

WHAT NATIVE TONGUE?

THE COLUMBUS Day debacle is just one example of the ever-expanding effort by the cult of multiculturalism to encourage people to forget our roots and downplay or destroy our heritage. So cult practitioners do things to deemphasize our society's uniqueness, such as working against any effort to officially adopt a common language.

English is America's "native tongue" and always has been, but the cult's influence over our politicians and national policies has led to our essentially telling millions of immigrants and first-generation Americans that they *shouldn't* learn English. Instead, we will teach their children in their native language.

In Mason, Ohio—twenty miles northeast of Cincinnati—a bar owner was forced to remove a sign from his window that read, "For Service, Speak English." The Ohio Civil Rights Commission ruled the sign was discriminatory against all "non-English speaking individuals," but was especially an "affront" to Hispanics because bar owner Tom Ullum said that Mexicans regularly frequented his establishment.[5] Apparently it didn't occur to anyone on the "civil rights" commission that Ullum had the right to be addressed in his own business and, more important, in a language he understood.

In Arizona, a state with a large Hispanic population, voters approved Proposition 203 in 2000, banning so-called bilingual education—rules that forced schools to teach children in their native language. Instead, voters mandated the adoption of English-immersion classes that required English-language instruction in all classrooms so the children could more quickly learn the language. Opponents sued, and in response, a federal court ordered the state to increase spending for English-language learners, estimated at about 160,000 kids statewide. But it didn't stop there. The influx of non-English-speaking children into Arizona has long been out of control, so the federally ordered costs to state residents continue to spiral up.

In New York City in early spring 2005, members of the city council proposed legislation that would *require,* within twenty-four hours, the "translation into at least nine languages . . . of school toilet passes, detention slips, and heaps of other documents spawned by the educational ministry."[6] Councilman Dennis Gallagher opposed the legislation, explaining that his concern centered around something more profound than just the cost of implementation: "Great nations, no matter how ethnically diverse, have a common bond that unites its people. . . . That common bond is language, and we shall do everything in our power to encourage that commonality rather than destroy it." For that, however, he was vilified as a "Nazi" and a "racist," though by any measure he was trying to bring sanity to the situation. Almost *two hundred* languages are spoken in New York City; so which *nine* are school officials supposed to choose? And why those *nine?*

About seventy languages are spoken in the Dallas, Texas, public school system, while 63 percent of primary-school students are Spanish-speaking. Because of that, in the summer of 2005, Dallas School Board trustee Joe May proposed a requirement that *all* district school principals learn Spanish. He said he got the idea after hearing complaints from parents after an awards ceremony at the Sam Houston Elementary School that the ceremony was *only in English.* "What I hope to accomplish," May told CNN, "is to make the system more acceptable to where they can deal with barriers that they often . . . have to encounter, and, therefore, be able to provide a better quality of education for that kid."[7] This ridiculous idea assumes that kids will do better in school with Spanish-speaking principals, though there is *no* evidence that would be the case.

THE HYPHENATED AMERICA

IN HIS 1991 book, *The Disuniting of America,* Arthur M. Schlessinger Jr., two-time recipient of the Pulitzer Prize and former special assistant to President John F. Kennedy, believed no one in the nineteenth century thought more carefully about representative government than John Stuart Mill. As Mill saw it, the two elements that defined a nation were the desire on the part of the inhabitants to be governed together and the common sympathy instilled by shared history, values, and language (in other words, a common *heritage*). Free institutions, Mill observed, are next to impossible in a country made up of different nationalities. "Among the people without fellow feeling, especially if they read and speak different languages, united public opinion, necessary for the working of representative government, cannot exist. It is in general a necessary condition of free institutions that the boundaries of government should coincide in the main with those of nationalities," said Mill.

This "disuniting" phenomenon is growing rapidly in our country. You can see it in the way we balkanize and divide ourselves into cultural and ethnic subgroups of hyphenated Americans. And as Schlessinger points out, lawmakers have helped usher in the current climate of dangerous multiculturalism:

> In 1974, after testimony from ethnic spokesmen denouncing the melting pot as a conspiracy to homogenize America, Congress passed the "Ethnic Heritage Studies Act"—a statute that, by applying the ethnic ideology to all Americans, compromised the historic right of Americans to decide their ethnic identities for themselves. The act ignored those millions of Americans—surely a majority—who refused identification with any ethnic group. The ethnic upsurge (it can hardly be called a revival because it was unprecedented) began as a gesture of protest against the Anglocentric culture. It became a cult, and today it threatens to become a counterrevolution against the original theory of America as "one people," a common culture, a single nation.[8]

I have sat in the House and listened to members of various ethnic caucuses speak, and I am concerned that we are doing things that will pull us apart and separate us into exclusionary groups both as individuals and as enemies. Some people say that America's diversity is its strength. While there are positive aspects of diversity, there are times when diversity is emphasized to the extreme and becomes a negative and divisive factor. When we are pulled apart and divided along ethnic lines—as opposed to ideological lines—I fear we are causing long-term damage to our society.

This was exemplified recently when I heard members of the Hispanic Caucus speak for an hour on the House floor, dutifully recounting the notable achievements of Hispanic Americans. I say dutifully because I thought it appropriate that those observations were made and those accomplishments were lauded. Nonetheless, as I listened to caucus members, it struck me how peculiar it is to have such a thing as a race-based caucus in Congress. Certainly these caucuses are not unique to Washington DC; there are state legislatures around the country, as well as public and private organizations, that branch off into similar subgroups. But this brings to mind the problem we are having in trying to integrate into our society all peoples of various ethnic origins.

To some extent, many people desire to integrate into our society and to do so as quickly as possible when they arrive as new immigrants to America. That's how it has been since the founding of our country. Most people who come to the United States come here for their own reasons; they want to adjust to the American scene by disassociating themselves from their past and by integrating themselves into the American mosaic. That's how it should be.

At first blush it seems natural for people of similar backgrounds and histories to form themselves into organizations that reflect their individual points of view and attitudes. But I believe it's peculiar to have similar organizations in Congress and in other legislative groups around the country. For more than 150 years, American leaders have tried to bring genuine equality to all our people. It is interesting that any thought of establishing a "white caucus" would justifiably be denounced as the epitome of racism.

All of this came to mind again when I was asked to speak to the Hispanic Human Resources Association in Denver. These individuals work in companies throughout the state as human resource and development professionals. Not surprisingly, the group wanted to talk to me about my position on immigration, a position that is very unpopular with a number of Hispanic organizations (but not so unpopular among many Americans of Hispanic origin who are negatively impacted by massive immigration). The other speaker was a non-Hispanic representative of a Democratic member of the U.S. congressional delegation from Denver.

At the conclusion of our discussions, a gentleman in the back of the room said that he was concerned about the fact that he and others in the audience did not believe they were represented by anyone at the dais. In other words, he was saying that neither the congresswoman nor I reflected his views, and this annoyed him.

His observation interested me greatly because it goes directly to what I am talking about regarding the ethnic caucuses in the House and the subdividing of our people into ethnic groups. I told him I was intrigued by his words because he insinuated that I could not effectively represent him since I am not Hispanic. It was not because we did not see eye to eye on the issues of taxation, Social Security reform, the degree of support for the military, or any of the wide variety of issues that come every day to the floor of the House of Representatives. He felt neither of us could represent him because neither of us was Hispanic.

In reply, I said, "Do you know what that means? It means you are telling me I cannot represent your interests because I am Italian. I may very well *not* represent your point of view on a wide variety of issues. If you are very liberal, and I am a conservative Republican, you are probably right that I do not represent your political point of view. I will give you that. But that has nothing to do with ethnicity. It is because I simply do not agree with your issues." I went on to question his assumption that my colleague also could not represent him because she is not Hispanic.

He responded, "Are you telling me you really think we should not have separate groups to represent our points?"

I said, "You're right, if what you are telling me is that your point of view needs to be represented by someone of a particular ethnic background. If so, then I am telling you that I am totally opposed to that."

I'm 100 percent Italian, but I would no more cast my vote for another American of Italian ethnicity simply because he or she was Italian than I would cast a vote blindly. For me, a candidate for office should represent my *views*, not my *hues*.

When I cast a vote for someone like Colorado Republican national committeewoman Lilly Nunez, I do so because her views are aligned with mine. If I were to live by the dictates of the Hispanic gentleman at the human resource meeting, or the people who come into Congress and form ethnic caucuses, or folks who gravitate to ethnic subgroups, I could not possibly vote for anyone other than white Italian Americans because no one else could represent my interests. How illogical is that?

THE WAR ON CULTURE

PERHAPS IT'S no surprise that leaders of organizations purportedly representing some of the country's largest ethnic groups have declared that they are in a culture war with America. One official of La Raza, the country's leading Hispanic "civil rights" organization, even told the *Fort Worth Star-Telegram*, "I think the biggest problem we have is a culture clash, a clash between our values and the values in American society."[9] It would be interesting to know just exactly what Mexican values he is talking about that are incompatible with American society.

Despite the obvious fallacy of this kind of narrow-minded thinking, lawmakers support and the courts continue to adjudicate congressional district lines that are drawn to "protect" specific minority groups so those groups can have their own representation. But that begs the question: Does the color of our skin affect our ability to respond to the needs, desires, wishes, and attitudes of our constituency? Do we actually believe that people who share the color of our skin can only represent us? In my opinion, that is a very dangerous attitude.

I don't blame my colleagues for extolling the virtues of Hispanic Americans. The people mentioned by the caucus members are indeed great people, and I certainly join them in praising their accomplishments. Perhaps one measure of our maturity as a nation will be when we feel comfortable with extolling the accomplishments of unhyphenated *Americans*. If our goal is to remain a United *States* of America, we must first be a united *people* of America.

After 9/11, I saw banners all over the country that proclaimed "United We Stand." So let's be united! That's a great message, and it's a very desirous goal. After 9/11, Americans were united as a people against the threat of international terrorism, which is exactly what we have to be. How does it help to be constantly reminded of our differences, be they ethnic, religious, or anything else? Doing so is detrimental to the interests of America.

I wonder what our Founding Fathers would say of these self-imposed divisions. I would be fascinated to know what they might have said if, during their deliberations on the Declaration of Independence and U.S. Constitution, someone had suggested it would be important to add provisions assuring that every identifiable ethnic group should congregate in designated areas so they could be fully represented by one of their own.

There can be disagreements over ideas and ideology, as evidenced by the divisions within the House of Representatives of right and left, conservative and liberal, Republican and Democrat. Those are good. But we should not be divided along racial and ethnic lines. No hyphenated Americans, please.

We are a country to which many people came from many different places. All had a common purpose: to join a new, exciting nation built not from conquest but on ideals, to participate in a new, exciting experiment in government. They came to seek a new life and, most important, to break ties with the Old World. When these millions of people came, the cultural and political forces of the times drove them into an amalgamation, a *melting pot*. But I sense it is no longer this way. For years I have witnessed a difference in both the kinds of immigration and the kinds of people who are coming to the United States. Too many new immigrants continue to be loyal to their native countries. They desire to maintain their own language, customs, and culture; yet they seek to exploit the success of America while giving back as little as possible in return. When massive numbers of people with those views come into the United States, the goals of cohesion and assimilation once reserved for immigrants seem more elusive than ever, especially when Native Americans are also looking to subdivide and hyphenate.

After teaching civics courses for eight years in Jefferson County, Colorado, I can attest to the fact that children are not born with an innate appreciation of the founding of America, the Declaration of Independence, the Bill of Rights, and who and what we were when we began as a nation. Children don't come equipped with history genes, so they don't understand these things instinctively or naturally. They have to be *taught*. The value of American principles, concepts, and ideals must not only be appreciated in schools, it must also be taught at home as well. Before children ever reach school age, they must have this exposure so educators can reinforce the founding principles of our nation.

Just as kids do not come with an inherent appreciation of art, literature, or music, they must learn to appreciate their American heritage. Children must learn what it means to be an American citizen and how being one separates us from the rest of the world. But few kids learn these things at home, and too many teachers don't teach it either.

Don't misunderstand me. When I talk about the problems multiculturalism has created for our society, I am not talking about the kind of cultural diversity that deepens our society with the music, poetry, art, dance, and foods from other parts of the world. Certainly, these contributions have enriched us as a nation. Nor am I talking about people who have brought their language and religion, for instance, into our free society. Nor am I talking about new immigrants who continue speaking their native tongue in their homes and want to pass it on to their children as part of their heritage. What I am talking about, however, is the current politically motivated drive to enshrine diversity as a goal that requires and demands a change in the fundamental American values that govern *our* civic institutions.

What the advocates of this new diversity seek is a kind of reverse assimilation. They want society to incorporate and adapt to the values of *other* cultures. They refuse to expect anyone to adopt what is already here. An example of this is the political drive to establish bilingualism as a national standard for government operations and commercial life. Previous immigrant generations expected their children to learn English. In the recent past, we have seen the rise of a political movement that seeks to perpetuate a parallel culture that does not speak English and thus cannot participate fully in the mainstream of American life. There were and still may be schools in our cities in which children are never taught in English. How can the children be expected to become full-time American citizens?

In his book, *The Marketing of Evil*, David Kupelian dissects multiculturalism to stunningly conclude:

> How strange. Out of the thousands of years of suffering that comprise human history, a light burns brightly for just a couple of hundred years. The American experiment: a revolutionary idea that the common man can be free, master of his own government, so long as he himself is ruled by God. For a short time this brilliant young country dazzles all the world and all of history, not just with its power and productivity and progress, but with its goodness. . . .
>
> The great melting pot—*e pluribus unum*—depended on an ideal. But the melting pot has become corrupted without this guiding spirit. Millions now residing here are not loyal to American values. Rather than unified and color-blind, the nation is divided and segregated. On top everything else, America literally has been invaded, and we are at war.[10]

If the current trends continue, our American heritage will be lost forever. If that happens, our civic culture and political institutions that have guaranteed "life, liberty, and the pursuit of happiness" to all will be gone as well. Only by uniting against those who seek to divide us will we preserve the Union.

3

Imparting the Cult of Multiculturalism

I certainly would not be the one to even suggest that a man cease to love the home of his birth and the nation of his origin. These things are very sacred and ought not to be put out of our hearts. But it is one thing to love the place where you were born, and it is another to dedicate yourself to the place to which you go. You cannot dedicate yourself to America unless you become in every respect and with every purpose of your will thoroughly Americans. You cannot become thoroughly Americans if you think of yourself in groups. A man who thinks of himself as belonging to a particular national group in America has not yet become an American, and a man who goes among you to trade upon your nationality is not worth to live under the stars and stripes.

—President Woodrow Wilson, addressing newly sworn-in American citizens in 1915

FOR SEVERAL YEARS THERE has been a rise in the influence of a self-destructive belief and behavior system I call the "cult" of multiculturalism—a subtle but potent shift in the attitudes espoused by many Americans. It is so pervasive it now permeates every segment of our society. It is creeping into our public schools and onto our college campuses. While this philosophy may be peculiar to most Americans, it is taking hold among elites, academics, the media, and certain groups within the political establishment.

This cult has been transformed from a rather benign philosophy of teaching an appreciation and a tolerance of differences to a malignant one that degrades and debases our uniquely American culture as well as Western civilization in general. It teaches our children that there is no value to who we are and what our country has accomplished in its short

230-year existence—except that *whatever* we've done has been bad or has had a negative impact on the world. I have often heard the United States criticized because, while the nation is only a small percentage of the world's population, it is the largest consumer of the world's resources. To the multiculturalists this is a bad thing; to me it is a success story. By any other measurement, we would hail such progress as an enormously positive accomplishment.

Let me emphasize that I do not believe we have never done anything wrong nor that Western civilization is a set of ideas and principles that developed without problems. Many of those ideals are not yet reached, so I am supportive of the thought that we have to teach our children the truth about who we are, warts and all. That said, I am extremely concerned that we concentrate so much of our teaching on asserting that there is nothing good about Western civilization or about the United States.

The cult of multiculturalism is at war with the idea of America that has been understood for more than two hundred years. In the 1940s and during the Second World War, Hollywood was looked upon as a bastion of patriotism. The movies of that era were patriotic in nature, and anyone who expressed patriotic feelings was not looked down upon by society as a whole. But something has dramatically changed since then. From the entertainment industry to our classrooms, people today are afraid to express their love of America for fear they will be shunned or ridiculed by their peers.

It is time to regenerate a discussion of American principles and ideas and to make everybody—our children and ourselves—understand their importance, because at this time we have been trained not to understand them.

More than a year ago, I was invited to speak to a group of students at a new high school in my district. I can assure you that what happened that day was much more of a learning experience for me than it was for them.

Approximately 250 students attended the gathering. My presentation and speech took about twenty minutes, and afterward some students submitted written questions. One read, "What do you think is the most serious problem facing the country?" I replied that I would answer that with a question of my own. So I asked how many believed that we lived in the greatest nation on earth. When I looked around, what I saw was incredible.

Remember, this happened in a suburban school district in Douglas County, Colorado. The area is full of middle- to high-income, predominantly white families. In a materialistic sense, they are living the American dream. Yet when I asked my question, only about two dozen kids raised their hands—about 10 percent—and most of them sheepishly. The rest of the student body just sat there. Some looked uncomfortable. I thought that some of them wanted to answer yes, but they seemed afraid to do so. They looked at their teachers, almost as if they were thinking, "Should I actually answer this? If I say yes, someone might challenge me, and I will have to defend myself." This is not only a problem in public schools, but also in the Christian schools I have visited.

I changed gears and asked another question: "Do you realize we are a product of Western civilization? How many of you would agree that this is something about which you can be proud?" At most, a dozen kids raised their hands, which prompted me to answer the original question. I told them I believed that one of the biggest problems facing America was exactly what was going on in that auditorium. I asked them to consider whether they had ever known, heard, or read about anyone who had ever fled *from* the United States for a better life in, say, Pakistan—or anywhere else for that matter? I then asked the same about anyone who has fled *to* the United States seeking the same thing? When they open the gates all over the world, people run in one direction: to Western civilization and to its epitome, the United States.

I know what happened was not unique to this suburban school in my district. I could have asked that question in any high school in America, and the response would have been similar: tepid, sheepish support, with most people saying, I don't know, I don't care, and what difference does it make?

In another school in my district just before Christmas, I was talking to a large number of fifth and six graders. When I left the room, I said, "Merry Christmas!" Again, there was an uneasy response, with only a few kids acknowledging me and saying, "Okay." As I was walking out, a teacher's aide said, "You know the principal does not like us using the word 'Christmas' here." As I pointed to a Christmas tree in the hallway, I asked, "What is that?" She said it was a "seasonal" tree. I replied, "Are you telling me that we cannot use 'Christmas'?" And she said, no, but the teachers don't. Not to be deterred, I waited until all the kids came out, and I very loudly wished them all a "Merry Christmas!" In reply, they all responded, "Merry Christmas!" This kind of thing is happening in schools all over the United States. This is not a situation that is unique to my little suburban district in Colorado. If parents went to their own schools to inquire about these things, they would no doubt be shocked by the answers coming from the school administrators and teachers.

My most recent experience with high-school students—and the most disconcerting—occurred in December 2005. I was asked by an advanced placement history teacher at Denver's East High School to speak to a couple of classes. Although Denver is not in my district, I agreed because I enjoy speaking to students and do my best to bring them a perspective regarding the values of our society that I don't believe they are exposed to very often. East is an old, inner-city school, and I wanted to see how the kids there would react to my query about their feelings toward their nation.

When I arrived at the school, it was just as the "holiday assembly" had been dismissed. The cacophony in the halls was deafening. I looked at a beleaguered lady sitting at a small desk near the front door to monitor who was entering and exiting the building. As students yelled greetings to each other at the top of their lungs and then wrapped themselves around each other in hello "hugs," the door monitor and I tried to communicate. She explained that it was always like that after assemblies. As she led me to the office where I needed to sign in, I noticed the walls and hallways were devoid of any "offending" Christmas decorations.

As students wandered into the auditorium-style classroom to which I had been escorted, I chatted with the teacher and was told that many students had boycotted the holiday assembly because they heard there was going to be a song with a religious connotation performed by the school's choir.

After a brief introduction, I immediately told the forty-four students and three teachers that I believed immigration was a very serious public policy issue and that I spent much of my time talking about it. A young man in the front row replied in an ominous tone, "We know." The ensuing discussion was similar to those I have had in scores of classrooms throughout the country over the last few years until I asked, "How many of you believe you live in the greatest country in the world?" Four students raised their hands. Although that is the same percentage of positive responders I get in other schools, the comments that the question engendered were disturbingly antagonistic and not typical of the reaction in other schools. Up to that moment, I had the impression that most of the kids who did not raise their hands did so out of ignorance, not out of feelings of malice toward their country. They were intellectually unable to affirm the proposition. The information they had been provided up till then was politically correct nonsense that avoided any possible complimentary reference to America. But these kids at East High were different. These students *knew* why they hated this country. The comments were filled with vitriol and animosity. To them, America was beset with racism, sexism, chauvinism, and just about every other ism that has a negative connotation. The real problems we faced, it seemed to them, were those perpetrated by religious, *Christian* fanatics like the "jerk" in Colorado Springs. (This was a reference to Dr. James Dobson, president of Focus on the Family, which is headquartered in Colorado Springs.) One young man said the reason we have problems with some aliens is because we do not do enough to accommodate their values. When I asked what we should do if some aliens came here with values that were antithetical to ours—like radical Islamists who want to set up a Caliphate—there was an immediate collective sneer. Suddenly, we reverted back to those damned Christians who were every bit as bad as radical Muslims.

At the end of the class, the teacher walked out with me. We talked outside the school for a few minutes. He expressed concern with the worldview of the students and reminded me that we were in the heart of Denver, a liberal bastion surrounded by conservative suburbs. He pointed out that what I had witnessed was probably more a reflection of the conversations that took place at the family dinner table than of public school pedagogy. But I have no doubt they are both.

I'll never forget the last thing the teacher told me that day. I mentioned that much of their anger and cynicism was focused on President

Bush. "Yes," he said. "Do you remember the quiet young man in the blue shirt?" he asked. Recently the teacher had mentioned to the class that the president would be in Denver for a fund-raising event. The quiet young man asked, with a degree of seriousness that made the teacher's blood run cold, "Will he be in range?"

I do not believe for a minute that these incidents are unique to my congressional district or in just a few districts around the country. I believe I could have asked any group of students anywhere in the country how they feel about their country, and the responses would have been the same or nearly the same: tepid, sheepish support or dismissive antipathy.

This is *not* natural. If I were to shout, "Hey, who has the best school?" these same students would have immediately shouted back, "We do!" If I were to shout, "Who has the best football team?" they would have shouted back, "We do!" even if they hadn't won a game all year. But when I asked, "Who lives in the greatest country on earth?" I get massive hesitation and palpable uncertainty. This is a "conditioned response," meaning it is a response these kids have been *taught*.

BLAME AMERICA FIRST

NOT LONG after 9/11, the National Education Association—the country's largest teachers' union—distributed some "suggestions" for teachers and parents, instructing them on how to address the issue of the attack on the United States. Not one word of the handout mentioned the uniqueness of America and the importance of defending the country. The entire descriptor was aimed at telling parents and children they should *not* think *negatively* about the people who attacked our country. That is to say, we should not use the attacks to cast aspersions on any groups or any organization because, after all, there are many bad things we have done too, and that maybe we brought the attack on ourselves.

In keeping with that theme, when former President Bill Clinton spoke on a college campus shortly after the attacks, he said essentially the same thing, adding that the reason America had been attacked was because of our history of slavery and our historical treatment of Native Americans.

I found it incredible that a former president would tell *anyone* that 9/11 was *our* fault. Even more incredulous is the fact that he is still held in high esteem by millions of Americans. But his example, as well as the NEA's admonition to refrain from holding anyone but Americans responsible for the attack, became part of a chorus of self-deluded elitists who have instinctively blamed America for whatever ills happen in the world.

The 9/11 attacks seemed to incite more than just left-wing political responses. Instead of the shock, horror, and outrage expressed by most other Americans, the attacks seemed to evoke a perverse sense of gratification on many colleges and universities. The nation had not yet had time to tally its dead before many of the countercultural elites renewed their assault on the American character.

One of the most well-known perpetrators of this fraudulent cult is Ward Churchill, the now-infamous and former head of the ethnic studies department at the University of Colorado in Boulder. He made headlines when, on the day after 9/11, he publicly praised the Islamic fanatics who had staged the terrorist attacks in New York and Washington DC. He even lauded the "gallant sacrifices" of the "combat teams" who struck the Pentagon and the World Trade Center, absurdly claiming that the victims of the attack got what they deserved:

> The [Pentagon] and those inside comprised military targets, pure and simple. As to those in the World Trade Center: Well, really. Let's get a grip here, shall we? True enough, they were civilians of a sort. But innocent? Gimme a break. They formed a technocratic corps at the very heart of America's global financial empire—the "mighty engine of profit" to which the military dimension of U.S. policy has always been enslaved—and they did so both willingly and knowingly. If there was a better, more effective, or in fact any other way of visiting some penalty befitting their participation upon the little Eichmanns inhabiting the sterile sanctuary of the twin towers, I'd really be interested in hearing about it.[1]

("Little Eichmanns" refers to Adolf Eichmann, a high-ranking Nazi official who was largely responsible for the logistics of Hitler's Final

Solution that made the Holocaust possible. Eichmann oversaw the identification and transportation of millions of people to the various Nazi concentration camps.)

Churchill, mind you, held a position of academic authority and was being paid a handsome salary to teach young adults to believe that the terrorism of 9/11 was justified because our ancestors managed to achieve unprecedented success. Their success, ironically, made it possible for Churchill to have his high-paying, influential job in a country in which he has the right to say these outrageous things.

Churchill's extremism was emulated by scores of other "academics" who found little fault in the assassins but plenty with the assassinated. "My primary anger is directed at the leaders of this country," declared Professor Robert Jensen of the University of Houston in an editorial response. "The attacks on the Pentagon and the World Trade Center are no more despicable than the massive acts of terrorism, the deliberate killing of civilians for political purposes that the U.S. government has committed in my lifetime. We are just as guilty."[2]

Other centers of academia have also sided with our enemies. At Columbia University in New York City, the spring 2006 course catalog indicated that anthropology professor Nicholas DeGenova—who called for a "million Mogadishus" (in reference to U.S. troops killed in a peacekeeping operation on October 3–4, 1993) and said, "The only true heroes are those who find ways that help defeat the U.S. military"—would teach a graduate class on "The Metaphysics of Anti-terrorism."[3] With so much venom directed toward the United States by academicians and administrators, it should surprise no one that students themselves would display much of the same resentment.

On one occasion, a University of Colorado professor told me that, after 9/11, most of his students said that they had no feelings of patriotism for their country and did not even think about America in patriotic ways. One student told him, "It's not a requirement that Americans blindly follow their country." It may be true that patriotism is *not* best demonstrated by following your country or your government blindly, but if you can't demonstrate a knowledge of and appreciation for our unique form of government, our Bill of Rights and Constitution, and our commitment to equality (regardless of ethnicity and sex), how can you make a judgment about when it is a good time, the "right time," to follow your country?

Not long ago an article in the *Denver Post* discussed the differences in attitudes of people today who are twenty years old or younger and people who are older than twenty with regard to patriotism and love of this country. It found that younger Americans seemed to know very little about America. They really had very little understanding of who we are as a nation, who we are as a people, and the principles upon which the nation was founded. Because of that, the article concluded, they did not understand the significance of 9/11.

After I read that story, I thought about a chant that was popular on college campuses during the latter part of the Vietnam War. In making a passing reference to North Vietnam's communist leader, Ho Chi Minh, the chant went, "Ho Ho Ho, Western Civ has got to go!" Well, these days, "Western Civ" has gone away. Fully 70 percent of the elite institutions of higher education in America have dumped the subject altogether from their required course list. Then again, if more "teachers" are like Ward Churchill, perhaps we are better off for the lack of curricula.

TEACHING OUR CHILDREN ANTI-AMERICANISM

A RATHER small group of left-wing academics and authors have transformed themselves into a force strong enough to cleanse textbooks, censor all aspects of the media, and force political speechwriters to nervously scan texts for the slightest hint of something that might *offend*. In its statement of philosophy, the National Association for Multicultural Education (NAME) believes "xenophobia, discrimination, racism, classism, sexism, and homophobia are societal phenomena that are inconsistent with the principles of democracy and lead to the counterproductive reasoning that differences are deficiencies." That sounds good, except that the cult's definition of what is racist, classist, and sexist is as dogmatic and closed-minded as anything they criticize.

A lot has changed since my childhood of growing up in Denver and attending St. Catherine's Elementary School and Holy Family High School. Then, I was *taught* about my heritage—who I was as well as my own history. If someone would have asked me then (and if someone asked me now) what is my heritage, I would say proudly and without hesitation, "I am an *American*." I had American heroes and looked to American figures and icons for my heritage. I'm talking about Thomas Jefferson, Abraham Lincoln, George Washington, and John Adams. These are the leaders with whom I connected because, even though my ancestors did not come to America aboard the *Mayflower*, I was unabashedly taught to be an *American*.

That approach differs dramatically from the concept of multiculturalism, which doesn't advocate assimilation of American culture. Multiculturalism *demands manufactured diversity* in every facet of our lives. It is driven by a competing political ideology, one that is at odds with our traditional principles. The stated purpose of this cultist movement—that it is necessary to foster "tolerance"—has nothing to do with accepting other cultures. Americans have always done that and will continue to do it. Rather, it is a movement to supplant American traditions and customs with non-American traditions and customs because, we are told, our traditions and customs are selfish, egocentric, and exclusive. That's just rubbish!

Jim Nelson Black summarized the insidiousness of this cult on our education system when he observed, "As we enter the 21st century, at least three generations of young Americans believe what they have been taught: that their own native land is populated by men and women who are homophobic, bigoted, misogynist, exploitative, environmentally insensitive, and morally corrupt. Politicians and public officials have failed to challenge the perpetrators of this ongoing educational fraud."[4]

At Los Angeles's Roosevelt High School, an eleventh-grade teacher told a nationally syndicated radio program that she "hates" the textbooks she's been told to use and the state-mandated history curriculum because they "ignore the students of Mexican ancestry." Because the students don't see themselves in the curriculum, the teacher has chosen to modify the curriculum by replacing it with activities like "mural walks," intended to "open the students' eyes to their indigenous culture." A friend of the teacher invited to help with the mural walk went on to tell the students that essentially there is nothing in the American experience that they should attach themselves to as students. American culture is white. It is Anglo-Saxon. It is not theirs, and they should never become a part of it.

In a school district in New Mexico, students were "learning" from a textbook called *500 Years of Chicano History in Pictures*. It was written "in response to the Bicentennial Celebration of the 1776 American Revolution, *and its lies* [emphasis added]." The authors said its stated purpose was to "celebrate our resistance to being colonized and absorbed by racist empire builders." The book describes the defenders of the Alamo as "slave owners, land speculators, and Indian killers," Davy Crockett as a cannibal, and the 1847 war with Mexico as an unprovoked U.S. invasion. The chapter headings include "Death to the Invader," "U.S. Conquest and Betrayal," "We Are Now a U.S. Colony," "In Occupied America," and "They Stole the Land." At least the authors can't be accused of resorting to subliminal messages.

In the Prentice-Hall textbook *America: Pathway to the Present*, students could be forgiven for getting the impression that U.S. armed forces were happily integrated and that people of color suffered and died in numbers equal to whites. The first five pages of the chapter on World War II focus on such topics as women in the armed forces and on the home front, racial segregation and the war, black Americans and the home front, and Japanese American internment. Some 292,000 Americans died in the conflict, almost all of them white, but in the school texts, white male soldiers are represented far less in photos and words than all others.[5]

The book's politically correct authors refer to South Vietnam president Ngo Dinh Diem's repression in his country but fail to reference the purge by communists in North Vietnam from 1951 to 1956 that killed about fifty thousand Vietnamese. It states that Vice President George H. W. Bush's 1988 ads attacking Democratic presidential nominee Michael Dukakis during the 1988 election created a nasty political contest and alienated voters while simultaneously contributing to low voter turnout. The textbook also discusses the introduction of Old World (read *Western*) diseases into the New World, but it does not discuss diseases brought back to Europe, such as a lethal strain of syphilis that killed many Europeans in the early 1500s. The authors go on to argue that traditional sex roles deny women full equality because they do not empower them to perform as men. It then fails to mention in the *brief* reference to Thanksgiving that the Pilgrims were thanking *God* for their good fortune in the New World.

Meanwhile, Holt-Reinhart-Winston's *American Nation in the Modern Era* includes an exercise that calls for students to criticize—but not defend—support for immigration restrictions in the 1800s (is it possible that some people during that time were concerned about anything other than the race of the people entering the United States?). The reference links anyone opposed to immigration reform to racism and implies such opponents are discriminating and intolerant.

The book devotes 1,456 lines to social protests by ethnic and other groups from the 1950s to the 1970s, but far fewer lines to the U.S. involvement in World Wars I and II—wars that liberated billions of people from the bonds of tyranny.

The 2002 textbook *American Odyssey,* published by McGraw-Hill and written by UCLA history professor Gary B. Nash, devotes as much space to James Madison, the father of the U.S. Constitution and the fourth president of the United States, as is given to Cesar Chavez. The 2002 guidelines for teaching history in the New Jersey public schools failed to mention the Founding Fathers, the Pilgrims, or the *Mayflower*— a gross error that was finally changed after public outcry. And *Michigan: The World Around Us* is a fourth-grade text that contains an uneven focus on specific groups. Its author, JoEllen Vinyard, tends to present minority groups as courageous heroes overcoming great obstacles. At the same time, it presents whites as miscreants and oppressors.

How did this sea change in attitudes come about? For one thing, multiculturalism's biggest worshipers have obviously infested the institutions that most influence the direction of our educational institutions. For another, they have made it nearly impossible to publicly refute them because they have been so effective in shaming their critics into silence.

Yet frustration is growing among teachers and faculty who understand, as I do, the kind of damage the cult of multiculturalism is causing to society. This annoyance was epitomized by a Los Angeles schoolteacher who told me that he was "deeply offended" to see American culture both ignored and desecrated. In his letter, he said that the middle school in which he taught had scheduled five "cultural celebrations" during the 2005 school year but did not plan any observances to mark traditional *American* events. Emphasis was placed on Latino Heritage Celebration, Dia de la Muertos ("Day of the Dead," an Aztec ritual), an Underground Railroad play (an observance of Harriet Tubman's efforts to aid runaway slaves during the time before the Civil War), Hawaiian Day, and the "Unity Festival," which was formerly known officially as Multicultural Day.

Noting there would be "more added to this list as the school year wears on," this teacher continued:

> February is Black History Month, which usually brings a veritable orgy of announcements extolling the achievements of blacks. African Dress Day (primarily by the black students and teachers) and the assembly, the grand finale, is always a pip. The whole school is treated to the joys of African culture including, on occasion, a fertility dance put on by eleven- to thirteen-year-olds. Actually, this latter event is good training, since a fair share of the students at my school will be intellectually equipped to be nothing more than exotic dancers when they leave Los Angeles Unified. . . .
> On a serious note, you will notice that no one celebrates our American heritage—Washington, Jefferson, Adams, Hamilton, and Lincoln are never mentioned. That "dead white male" thing is alive and well in public education. Veterans Day? It's a good day to go to the mall. The schools are closed but no one will tell you why. Flag Day? It is known at my school as "June 14."

As to Memorial Day, the teacher said he "dutifully" gets on the school's public address system to "explain to those who will listen" what the observance is all about. He says he reads students a list of military men and women who work at the school and asks them to thank them for their service. But that's all that happens. "No speeches, no essays, no assemblies, and no acknowledgment of the importance of fighting for your country."

Syndicated columnist Suzanne Fields notes that, even in the war on terror, the countercultural elites portray America as the bad guy:

One man's jihad can be another man's mission of distortion. A lot has gone missing from our textbooks. *Patterns of History,* for example, published by Houghton Mifflin and adopted as a world history textbook in high-school classes in Texas and other states, never even mentions the word *jihad.* A seventh-grade world history book by Houghton Mifflin, titled *Across the Centuries,* defines *jihad* merely as a struggle for a Muslim "to do one's best to resist temptation and overcome evil." There's no mention of the fact that millions of Muslims—not all, but many millions—are taught to regard everything not under Muslim rule or control as "evil."[6]

Since my earliest days as a teacher, I have found it deeply saddening to see an increasing number of American children experience a fear of extolling the virtues of their own country. It has been equally disturbing to see so many of them brainwashed into thinking that any praise of America will bring them ridicule and criticism. This self-defeatism and self-loathing of our cultural roots is destroying the fiber of our country as it destroys the students' future ability to enjoy the fruits of the world's most successful experiment in freedom and liberty.

There is no arguing the fact that the politically correct vendors of multiculturalism have intimidated teachers, education administrators, curriculum planners, textbook writers, and school boards into adopting badly revised and wholly incorrect versions of American history. There is also no disputing that such revisionist history also means our kids have almost no chance to hear an accurate depiction of our country's history—of *their* history. And the effects are noticeable.

Although I have few tools at my disposal to respond to this phenomenon, to that end I have proposed a congressional resolution stating that students graduating from American schools should be able to articulate an appreciation for Western civilization. It doesn't mandate anything on our schools or demand we change our textbooks. The resolution just says that we believe, as a body, that children graduating from our schools should be able to articulate an appreciation for Western civilization. I think it's an important first step. It's not too late.

As I ponder our future, I often recall a popular poem I learned in high school: Thomas Macaulay's "Horatius at the Gate." The poem recounts a time when barbarians besieged ancient Rome. Needless to say, there was great panic and fear throughout the city. But the story told of a young man, Horatius, who bravely volunteered to defend a bridge that separated Rome from the invading horde. Horatius took two friends with him. The bridge they guarded was a narrow span, and they were determined to defend it until their compatriots could pull down the bridge on the other side, leaving the three defenders at the mercy of the barbarians. Macaulay wrote:

> Then out spake brave Horatius,
> The Captain of the Gate:
> "To every man upon this earth
> Death cometh soon or late.
> And how can man die better
> Than facing fearful odds,
> For the ashes of his fathers,
> And the temples of his gods."[7]

We are committing cultural suicide. Worse, by the time many of us recognize it, our country may itself be so weakened by these destructive influences that the barbarians at the gate will only need to give a slight push, and the emaciated body of Western civilization will collapse in a heap.

To quote historian Will Durant: "If Rome had not engulfed so many men of alien blood in so brief a time, if she had pressed all those new-comers to her schools instead of her slums, if she'd occasionally closed her gates to let assimilation catch up with infiltration, she might have gained new racial and literary vitality from the infusion, and might indeed have remained a Roman Rome."[8]

4

Adopting Bilingualism

Uɴᴅᴇʀ ᴛʜᴇ ᴅɪʀᴇᴄᴛɪᴏɴ ᴏғ the recently departed city librarian, Rick Ashton, the Denver Public Library (DPL) has developed a radical plan to convert several of its twenty-three branches into bilingual libraries with large Spanish-language holdings. Spanish will be a required language for all newly hired staff, and new acquisitions in those branches will be heavily weighted to Spanish-language materials. These changes are aimed at serving what the library management calls Denver's "new arrivals." The new plan for the DPL assumes these "new arrivals" must be served in their native language.

DPL leaders always refer to these new arrivals as "immigrants," making no distinction between legal immigrants and "undocumented" immigrants. Since the days of Mayor Wellington Webb, city officials have always spoken approvingly of Denver's "welcoming attitude" toward "all immigrants," illegal aliens included. Thus, the new direction being taken by the DPL is in keeping with the "sanctuary city" policies established by Webb and followed by his successor, John W. Hickenlooper.

There are two distinct aspects of this change in direction by the city library: the plan itself and how it was imposed on the community by library management. The basic goal of establishing bilingual branch libraries with prominent Spanish-language sections was first developed by the library staff in 2002 and 2003, but the plan needed to be sold to a skeptical public. Employing professional consultants for polling and marketing and utilizing ten focus groups, seven "community conversations," and the library's forty-three-member advisory committee, the plan went forward in 2005.

Contrary to the library's news releases, the plan was not the *product* of these community conversations. Ashton and his management team used the focus groups and community meetings to market the plan to the public, but the key elements of the plan were never changed, and criticisms of the plan were either deflected or ignored. The "community input" project orchestrated by DPL in 2005 was a charade.

THE USE AND ABUSE OF STATISTICS

FORMER CITY librarian Ashton and DPL management have consistently justified the movement to bilingual libraries as a response to "changing demographics." The document used to impress skeptics was a September 2001 study commissioned by the library: *Demographics of Immigration in Metro Denver and Colorado, 2001: Implications for Public Library Services.* That study concludes with this assertion: "The library has a civic responsibility to serve all its constituents and to reach out to everyone in the community, especially the newest arrivals and those who speak languages other than English. We must make every effort to attract the newcomers to the library, educate them about our resources, and make them regular customers [page 9]."

Among the study's findings were:

- A majority of Denver public school students (53.14 percent) are now Hispanic.
- Newcomers of Hispanic origin accounted for 75 percent of Denver's population growth in the 1990s.
- Nine percent of Colorado's population in 2001 was foreign-born, compared to 4.3 percent in 1990.

The demographic data summarized in the report is interesting, yet none of it explains in any meaningful sense why the "new arrivals" need to be served in Spanish or why they are likely to become library patrons. Nor does it explain why DPL should prefer them as customers if it means reducing services to other library customers. In fact, one piece of information found in the report that is pertinent to this question was virtually ignored: "A recent nationwide study of home language use by Hispanic students found that 57% speak mostly English at home, 25% speak mostly Spanish, and 17% speak both languages equally."

The 2001 report's conclusions and recommendations totally ignored the implications of this finding. If 74 percent of Hispanic students speak English at home or speak English and Spanish equally, where is the imperative to expand Spanish-language holdings to attract them to the library? DPL planners must have had some other constituency in mind because their plan will not improve services to the city's Hispanic students.

The item cited most often in DPL presentations to the public was that "over 20% of Denver families now speak Spanish at home." That is true, but it is a half truth. Three-quarters of those families also speak English at home!

Thus there is a very large disconnect between the demographic data in the report and the plan adopted by library management. There is no factual basis for the DPL conclusion that the city's Hispanic residents could *only* be attracted to the library by offering materials and services in Spanish. The important distinction here is that library management decided to focus its plan, not on Hispanic *residents* of Denver, but on Denver's *new arrivals*—namely, illegal aliens, who, in the judgment of the library management, do not want to learn English.

The question that was never posed in any of the public meetings held to explain and sell the program was: How important is it for the Denver Public Library to serve illegal immigrants who do not want to learn English if it means a commensurate decrease in services to other residents?

THE BILINGUALISM LOBBY

ONE REASON for the library management's commitment to the conversion plan may be found in its ideological commitment to bilingualism.

Former librarian Ashton and several other DPL employees are members of Reforma, a national organization of professional librarians who have adopted an activist agenda of bilingualism. Their program is described on the group's Web site (www.reforma.org).

> REFORMA has actively sought to promote the development of library collections to include Spanish-language and Latino oriented materials; the recruitment of more bilingual and bicultural library professionals and support staff; the development of library services and programs that meet the needs of the Latino community; the establishment of a national information and support network among individuals who share our goals; the education of the U.S. Latino population in regards to the availability and types of library services; and lobbying efforts to preserve existing library resource centers serving the interests of Latinos.

After Ashton's and his colleagues' association with Reforma were discussed on a Denver radio talk show, the Reforma Web site suddenly dropped the membership list from the site. Yet the Denver Public Library continues to be listed as an institutional member.

Several Hispanic organizations in Denver actively support and lobby for the move toward Spanish-language materials and bilingualism in library services. The weekly Spanish-language newspaper *La Voz Nueva* regularly features front-page stories promoting DPL's expansion of Spanish-language services. The August 24, 2005, issue was typical. A front-page story announced, "MOP Wants Library Help for Latino Families." (MOP refers to the Metropolitan Organization for the People.) What kind of help was being request and for which families?

According to the newspaper, "MOP released last Friday a portion of a larger research produced by the University of Denver about the need of library services for monolingual Spanish-speaking families."

What is important here is the emphasis on "monolingual Spanish-speaking families." MOP and its aficionados at *La Voz Nueva* are not simply dedicated to serving all Hispanic families or even all low-income Hispanic families. Their main emphasis is on providing city services *in the Spanish language*. They promote bilingualism among Spanish-speaking populations and government institutions like public schools and the public libraries, but they see nothing wrong with remaining monolingual if you are a Spanish-speaking family.

With the vocal support of many of the city's Hispanic organizations and the nodding acceptance of the city's political leadership, the conversion of many branch libraries to "Language and Learning Centers" with large Spanish-language holdings replacing English-language materials continues at the pace dictated by the plan originators.

AVOIDING AN HONEST DEBATE ON BILINGUALISM

IN OCTOBER 2005, Rick Ashton announced his retirement from the DPL, effective February 28, 2006. It is probably too much to expect that the mayor and his library commission will see Ashton's departure as an opportunity to reexamine the rush to bilingualism and to chart a new course that better serves the needs of *all* of Denver's residents. The mayor, the city council, and the DPL advisory committee might consider, for example, whether the city's public schools' struggle with very high dropout rates among Hispanic students is helped or hindered by sending a message that neither parents nor students need to learn English in order to use the public libraries.

Shortly after announcing his retirement, Ashton addressed the City Club of Denver. In the course of his remarks, he summarized the process of "public outreach" by using focus groups and community conversations and his advisory committee. He said that the process was listening to "what people actually tell us they need." He then summarized what the library managers learned from the series of public meetings on the bilingual issue: "During the past year, we have been testing some new ideas for service models. . . . Families with kids, single adults, English language learners all have differing needs and come to us for different things in different ways."

His only reference to the *language* of library materials and services is strangely vague, given the public controversy his plan had sparked. But the striking thing about this public summary of his proposal is this: Ashton characterized the large population of "new arrivals" whose existence gave impetus to the planned library transformation not as

Spanish-speaking individuals but as "English learners." Why? Calling the new (hoped-for) customers "English learners," even as his minions plow ahead with his plan to remove huge amounts of English-language materials and replace them with Spanish-language materials, was a tacit admission that his plan could not survive close scrutiny.

Ashton did not take time to explain to the City Club audience—and has never explained to anyone—how his plan will help those "new arrivals" become more successful "English language learners." Ashton wanted his audience to believe the purpose of this change is something all Denver citizens would applaud, especially Denver's business leaders: to help bring Spanish-speaking immigrants into the mainstream of society through the learning of English.

Listening to Ashton's description of his plan, a naive observer might assume that a "bilingual library" is one designed to help Spanish-speaking immigrants become *bilingual*—that is, to learn English. This idea was planted in the public mind by many DPL presentations. The possibility that Ashton's plan more likely will have the *opposite* result by removing incentives to learn English was never discussed at a single library commission or city council meeting.

Although Ashton did not take time in his City Club speech to describe his plan accurately, he did find time to lash back at his critics. He complained about how "opportunistic politicians and media figures" had attacked the library "for our exploration of the library service needs of Spanish-speaking Denver residents." Adding, "Amidst the hubbub was buried the not-so-subtle, exclusive idea that the freedoms and privileges we enjoy in this great city should somehow be withheld from many immigrants, that sizable portion of our population who have come most recently [to our city]."

Ashton's own words reveal the smear and the diversion attempted by DPL spokesmen against the critics of the Spanish-language conversion plan. In Ashton's view, anyone who believes as I do, that Hispanics and all Denver residents are better served by resisting bilingualism in library holdings and services, is simply against immigrants and against freedom. Ashton never acknowledged that there could be any honest or principled reason for opposing bilingualism. Could it be that the public officials who continually pander to the bilingual lobby in search of Hispanic votes and ethnic-based awards are the true "opportunistic politicians"?

The simple truth is that each step taken to make Denver's educational and cultural institutions more bilingual diminishes the incentives to learn English, a skill all immigrants need in order to advance economically in our country and to become full participants in civil life. For example, poor language skills are consistently noted in correlation to school dropout rates. Does the DPL management feel any responsibility to assist the public schools in fighting illiteracy and scandalously high dropout rates? How can the DPL claim to be a part of this effort while it is sending the opposite message by converting branches in Hispanic neighborhoods to institutions where English need not be spoken?

THE CONVERSION PLAN IN ACTION

THE SPANISH conversion plan was first announced to DPL staff in a November 2003 memo, but there were few details. The conversion plan is supposedly based on "demographic changes" in Denver, but there have also been meetings with the Mexican consul and some Latino activist groups. The plan is explained and marketed to the public as an "outreach to new constituencies," yet strangely, no survey of library patrons has been conducted to justify this change in focus.

A long-range goal that is key to the DPL plan is to get a new library district and a mill levy approved by voters to give the library a source of funds separate from the city's general fund and thus give the city librarian more freedom from city council oversight. The mill levy has been opposed by the mayor but is being kept alive in DPL planning documents. The creation of a predominantly Spanish-language West Denver branch (the "Latino Legacy Project") is part of the plan.

Major sections of branch libraries are now being converted to "reflect the language makeup of the local community," but this applies only to Spanish-speaking communities. Library management has ignored the fact that the majority of Denver's Spanish-speaking legal residents are bilingual and have not requested this conversion of English materials to Spanish materials.

Large quantities of books and materials in English are being thrown

59

out to make room for Spanish-language books and materials. After the Denver weekly *Westword* caught the library ditching books into Dumpsters in 2003, disposal methods were changed. Many books are now stored in boxes marked "Trash" in locked areas, then picked up surreptitiously after hours to be disposed of quietly. While it remains official library policy that all discarded books are first offered to schools and nonprofit organizations or saved for the library's biannual book sales, this is not how things are actually being done in the affected branches.

SELLING THE PLAN

DPL ANNOUNCED in 2003 a series of town meetings to get feedback on its strategic plan, but the series was canceled after three meetings. DPL then hired the Ciruli polling company and others to advise it on how to sell the mill levy. The Corona Research Group was retained to do research and organize focus groups. Ten focus groups were conducted in 2005 to gauge community reaction on the conversion plan, with two of them conducted in Spanish with translators for the non-Spanish-speaking members. Significantly, the last of the focus groups, held at the Woodbury branch and publicized widely by Spanish-language radio stations and newspapers as a forum for Spanish-speaking residents, had a total citizen participation of zero. Only the two translators showed up!

DPL also conducted a series of seven open houses to promote "community conversations" over the summer to sell the new plan. Yet, despite all the planning and professional publicity, the feedback from the community groups and structured focus groups was decidedly mixed, with no clear mandate for the conversion to Spanish-language holdings. The comment and question cards submitted by citizens at the community meetings were never shared with the library commission or the mayor.

DPL also held four advisory committee meetings during the spring and summer of 2005 to get supposed feedback and examine the results of the seven community conversations. The group consisted of community and business leaders handpicked by library management and expected to be supportive of library projects. The advisory committee originally consisted of fifty members, but several resigned rather than participate in the charade being perpetrated by library management. Library employees other than those selected by DPL management were forbidden to attend the advisory committee meetings.

Yet even this handpicked group of library supporters balked at signing a draft report on the community conversations that downplayed opposition to the plan. That report was never brought to a vote, and the library commission received it without being told that the advisory committee had not voted on it. This is but one example of how library management manipulated "public input" to get desired results.

During this marketing period, library employees were forbidden to talk to the public or library patrons about the new "Language and Learning" conversion plan for the branch libraries. Only top management and its public relations consultants were permitted to address the media or the public about the plan.

As mentioned earlier, Ashton and his team also have a plan for three new branch libraries to be funded by a mill levy—if they can get the levy on the city ballot and approved by the voters. Two of the new branches are slated for areas with rapid population growth, but the third is planned for the west side of Denver and designated as the home of the Latino Legacy Project. Library management hopes to generate a huge Hispanic vote in support of the mill levy and the three new branch libraries.

The basic idea for the Latino Legacy Project is reasonable and laudable—if it is in fact a section of a branch library housing a collection of historical records, photographs, memorabilia, and narrative describing the city's Hispanic heritage. But if it becomes instead a focal point for cultural separatism as the heart of an all-Spanish branch library, it will be a divisive force and a symbol of institutional collapse.

Here are a few examples of how far the conversion to Spanish-language bilingual libraries had progressed by November 2005, despite the fact that the plan had not yet been formally adopted by the library commission.

- DPL now conducts classes for Spanish-speaking residents on how to get a home loan through the Colorado Housing Assistance Corporation (CHAC). You do not have to be a legal resident of

Colorado or have a valid Social Security number (or even a library card) to participate in the classes.

- You need not be a legal resident or visa holder to get a library card. You don't need a passport, either; a Mexican driver's license will suffice. The written policy requiring proof of residence is not followed for Spanish-speaking customers seeking a library card, despite what the mayor may have been told by library management.

- A DPL senior manager announced to employees that she wanted to use part of a five-hundred-thousand-dollar federal grant to fund Spanish-language training for employees and to send staff to Spain and Mexico to learn Spanish.

- It was recently announced—verbally, not in writing—that all library employees must be fluent in Spanish before they can be considered for a promotion.

- No one who cannot speak Spanish is being interviewed for any job opening at any of the twenty-three branches if the job involves contact with the public.

- The priority placed on acquiring Spanish-language holdings has neglected other language holdings. In recent years, a policy decision was made to discard all other foreign-language holdings and concentrate solely on Spanish-language materials.

- DPL management has sought ways to skirt a 2003 state law *prohibiting* the acceptance of the Mexican government's "matricula consula" card as identification for any publicly supported service. That includes access to library cards. DPL asked the city attorney for an opinion regarding its acceptance of the matricula consula card. The request was declined.

- DPL accepts Mexican driver's licenses as adequate ID to use the library facilities. Employees are instructed not to ask questions of patrons with a Mexican driver's license; they are to "just take it." Since no attempt is made to verify the authenticity of a foreign driver's license, it is very easy for anyone to use a fake driver's license to get full access to all library books, videos, and other materials.

- Library management has recently announced to employees that in 2006 it will implement "after-hours computer labs" for Spanish-speaking residents. Spanish-speaking patrons will be allowed to use ten to twenty library computers to write e-mail messages and engage in chat rooms in order to communicate with family and friends anywhere in the world. These after-hours labs are not "English classes"—they will not promote increased proficiency in English. They are simply a service for Spanish-speaking residents being added at the same time that library hours for the general public are being reduced.

What kinds of Spanish-language materials will replace the English-language holdings being removed? Maybe we can get a preview by looking at the library's most famous Spanish-language acquisition efforts.

These little illustrated books were first brought to public attention in July 2005 by Denver radio talk-show host Peter Boyles. He revealed that DPL was spending thousands of dollars annually to purchase the comic book–style publications that graphically portray sex and violence against women. The booklets were easily accessible to children.

After the library first denied the charge and then tried to minimize the extent of the holdings, a library commission task force was appointed to investigate the matter. The task force determined that ten of the fourteen *fotonovela* series (70 percent) were unsuitable for DPL use and recommended their removal. The task force did not tell the commission that many of the branch library staff had complained for years about those materials; their objections were ignored by library management. More than six thousand booklets had been purchased with taxpayer funds over a thirteen-year period.

MARCHING TOWARD MULTICULTURALISM

MANY PROFESSIONALS among the library staff have voiced opposition to these ideologically and politically driven changes, but top management has suppressed their objections. As a result of Rick Ashton's autocratic management style, many library employees have left DPL for suburban libraries where bilingualism is not yet an issue, where traditional library services are still given top priority, and where volunteers are still welcomed and appreciated. There are no Mexican *fotonovelas* in the libraries of Aurora, Golden, Lakewood, or Littleton, and you don't need to speak Spanish to serve a Vietnamese patron.

The most distressing and disappointing thing about the planned fragmentation and politicization of the Denver Public Library is that no one in the civic establishment, Democrat or Republican, has had the courage to challenge it. The city council has been silent. Denver's two daily newspapers have supported the bilingual conversion process, first by ridiculing my criticism as "alarmist" and then by covering the story superficially.

The city's watchdogs have not barked while a vital educational and cultural institution has been converted into a bilingual institution to serve a political agenda and a balkanized community. Citizens ought to be alarmed, but instead they have been lulled to sleep by sophomoric euphemisms. Such is the power of political correctness among Denver's political, civic, and media elites these days.

5

Clash of the Civilizations

If you know the enemy and know yourself, you need not fear the results of a hundred battles. If you know yourself but not the enemy, for every victory gained you will suffer a defeat. If you know neither the enemy nor yourself, you will succumb in every battle.

—Sun Tzu

I REMEMBER READING Samuel Huntington's book *Clash of Civilizations* about eight years ago and thinking that it was interesting. After 9/11, I reread it and found it profound and prophetic. Huntington uses Kishore Mahbubani's phrase to describe all present global conflict as being between "the West and the rest." It is also true that almost everywhere on the globe, where Islamic countries are adjacent to non-Islamic countries, there is conflict. Muslims believe they must spread the word by mouth and by sword.

It was during this time that I came to believe the United States and Western civilization were in a "clash of civilizations." And it is a real clash . . . a real war. There are times when the conflict becomes very violent and times when it subsides. But the clash is real, and it promises to be here for some time. This view of the current conflict is not acceptable conversation in politically correct circles. And although I believe it is understood in the White House, it is not articulated there either. President George W. Bush continues to refer to our enemy as terrorism or, more recently, extremism. Of course, neither of these isms accurately characterizes our enemy. The real enemy is Islamofascism. Contrary to popular belief, Islamofascism did not begin with our support for Israel, and it would not end if that support were withdrawn.

In a very poetic speech given by Winston Churchill in 1899, the future British prime minister's insights regarding radical Islam are as relevant today as they were then:

> How dreadful are the curses which Mohammedanism lays on its votaries! Besides the fanatical frenzy, which is as dangerous in a man as hydrophobia in a dog, there is this fearful fatalistic apathy.
>
> The effects are apparent in many countries. Improvident habits, slovenly systems of agriculture, sluggish methods of commerce, and insecurity of property exist wherever the followers of the Prophet rule or live.
>
> A degraded sensualism deprives this life of its grace and refinement: the next of its dignity and sanctity. The fact that in Mohammedan law every woman must belong to some man as his absolute property, either as a child, a wife, or a concubine, must delay the final extinction of slavery until the faith of Islam has ceased to be a great power among men.
>
> Individual Moslems may show splendid qualities, but the influence of the religion paralyzes the social development of those who follow it.
>
> No stronger retrograde force exists in the world. Far from being moribund, Mohammedanism is a militant and proselytizing faith. It has already spread throughout Central Africa, raising fearless warriors at every step; and were it not that Christianity is sheltered in the strong arms of science, the science against which it had vainly struggled, the civilization of modern Europe might fall, as fell the civilization of ancient Rome.[1]

The clash of civilizations is not with the religion of Islam, but with the Islamic religion that has been married to a political philosophy that says that all nonbelievers must be annihilated, abolished, eliminated. It is with people who have openly and repeatedly stated that their desire is to kill you and your children, me and my children, to eradicate us from the planet because we do not accept their political and religious ideologies.

There is empirical proof that the basic tenets and characteristics of Islam are a cause for concern. In his book, *The Dunces of Doomsday*, Paul Williams clearly lays out the basic lessons of Islam and the Prophet Mohammed to convey our desperate need to understand our enemy.

- *Jihad is a religious duty.* . . ."Fight those who believe not in Allah nor the Last Day, nor hold that forbidden which hath been forbidden by Allah and his Messenger, nor acknowledge the religion of truth, [even if they are] the People of the Book [Christians and Jews], until they pay with willing submission and feel themselves subdued. . . ." (The Koran, 9:29).
- *Martyrdom is the highest good.* "Allah purchased of the believers their persons and their goods; for theirs in return is the Garden of Paradise: they fight in His cause, and slay and are slain: a promise binding on Him in truth" (The Koran, 9:111).
- *Muslims engaged in jihad must not show tolerance toward nonbelievers.* "Slay the idolaters wherever you find them" (The Koran, 9:5).
- *Acts of Terrorism . . . are justified by the Prophet's example.* "I will inspire terror in the hearts of Unbelievers: you smite them above their necks and smite all their fingertips off them" (The Koran, 8:2).[2]

Religious freedom is not permitted in the Islamic world. In Muslim countries, conversions can only go one way: from whatever you are to Islam. Punishment for the reverse procedure is torture or death. During an official visit to Egypt, I was part of a group that met clandestinely with representatives of the Coptic Christian community. They pled with us to urge their government to allow them to repair their churches and perhaps even build new ones. We then met with three Christian converts from Islam who had escaped after being imprisoned and tortured. They showed us their scars and told us their stories. Since then, I have met hundreds of Christians all over the world who have suffered the same fate.

Many scholars believe that Islam is incapable of a radical transformation. Many are skeptical about the possibility or the willingness of the vast number of righteous Muslims to reject radicalism in favor of a worldview in which Islam exists harmoniously with all other religions.

Father Joseph Fessio, provost of Ave Maria University in Naples, Florida, recently recounted on a radio program the observations of Pope Benedict XVI on the subject of radical Islam. In a dialogue with an Islamic scholar, the pope (then Cardinal Joseph Ratzinger) disputed the claim that a transformation of Islam was likely, because it would require a radical reinterpretation of the Koran. This could never happen because Muslims view the Koran as a document that cannot be interpreted by man.

In that same interview, Father Fessio discussed the demographic changes in Europe that will eventually lead to the United States' standing alone in the defense of Christianity and indeed Western civilization.

It isn't mentioned in polite company, but it is a well-known and accepted fact in the halls of power in the United States that we are at war—like it or not—with radical Islam. What's more, we know that Islam's most extreme practitioners are inextricably linked to terrorism and that terrorism will continue to be their preferred mode of warfare for years to come. So, despite the ten-second sound bites offered up for nightly news broadcasts by partisan hacks and mindless flacks, we must all be aware of the enemy: who they are, what they believe, why they believe it, and what they are prepared to do to carry out their aggression.

In fact, I have yet to meet anyone who does not believe the need to defend our homeland is greater now than it has ever been. There is rarely a day that goes by when Americans aren't exposed, in some form, to the horrors of terrorism committed in the name of radical Islam. Whether it is the images of what remains after a suicide bomber has detonated his backpack of death in a distant country or the audio from leaders of terrorist groups chanting, "Death to America," most of us believe that future attacks are more than likely. Today's technology provides our enemies with the ability to strike at us regardless of the vast oceans that separate our homelands.

In the immediate aftermath of the 9/11 attacks, noted constitutional attorney, best-selling author, and columnist Ann Coulter observed:

> After the World Trade Center was bombed by Islamic fundamentalists in 1993, the country quickly chalked it up to a zany one-time attack and 5 minutes later decided we were all safe again. We

weren't then. We aren't now. They will strike again. Perhaps they will wait another 8 years. Perhaps not. The enemy is in this country right now. And any terrorists who are not already here are free to emigrate. The government has been doing an excellent job in rounding up suspects from the last two attacks. But what about the next attack? We thought there was only one murderous Islamic cell in America the last time. Incorrect. Congress has the authority to pass a law tomorrow requiring aliens from suspect countries to leave. As far as the Constitution is concerned, aliens, which is to say any non-citizens, are here at this country's pleasure. They have no constitutional right to be here. Congress has, within its power, the ability to prevent the next attack, but it won't. When the Sears Tower is attacked, the president is assassinated, St. Patrick's Cathedral is vaporized, anthrax is released in the subway systems or Disneyland is nuked, remember: Congress could have stopped it, but didn't.[3]

If only our political and cultural leaders possessed Coulter's clarity of thought. If only we could see the "coalition of the willing" form to fight the battle of civilizations in which I believe we are engaged. If only we all understood that it is a fight to the death.

Awhile back, I spoke to a group of marines and their families before the troops were to ship out to Iraq. I thanked their families and loved ones for providing the moral support that would sustain these brave young men and women during the trying months that lay ahead and wished them godspeed and promised we would all be praying for their safe return. I would have given anything to have been able to assure our soldiers that we would be doing everything possible to protect their loved ones from attacks on the homeland. Unfortunately, I could not, in good conscience, relay this wish.

But I came home bursting with pride in the incredible young people who have resisted the siren songs of the cult and who have made a commitment to serve in their country's military. At the same time, I was heartsick because we have become so paralyzed by the cult that we refuse to see the enemy for who it is and refuse to take the steps necessary to confront every aspect of the threat it poses.

I will certainly grant that all of the world's billion and a half Muslims are not aligned with the likes of Osama bin Laden, that only a small percentage would strap on a bomb to detonate on a school playground. I must admit, however, I do wonder how many in the Muslim world are secretly pleased when they hear of such an attack. Judging from the tepid reaction to these events by the leaders of the Islamic world, I have to believe the number of sympathizers reaches into the hundreds of millions.

"DEATH TO AMERICA"

OF COURSE, many of those same leaders have given credence to Huntington's theory. Sheikh Abd al-Rahman al-Sudayyis of the Grand Mosque of Mecca, one of Islam's most sacred sites, believes and teaches:

> The most noble civilization ever known to mankind is our Islamic civilization. Today, Western civilization is nothing more than the product of its encounter with our Islamic civilization in Andalusia [medieval Spain]. The reason for [Western civilization's] bankruptcy is the reliance on the materialistic approach, and its detachment from religion and values. [This approach] has been one reason for the misery of the human race, for the proliferation of suicide, mental problems and for moral perversion. Only one nation is capable of resuscitating global civilization, and that is the nation [of Islam].[4]

Al-Sudayyis, who is the highest imam appointed by the Saudi government, also called for "Muslims to humiliate the infidels [non-Muslims]." His sermons, which spew hatred and call for the destruction of Jews and other enemies of Islam, are widely heard across the Middle East.

Dr. Yusef Al-Qaradawi, a controversial Egyptian imam who has been vetted by no less than Ken Livingstone, the mayor of London, has said, "For us, Muslim martyrdom is not the end of things but the beginning of the most wonderful of things." Al-Qaradawi, also the spiritual chieftain of the hard-line Muslim Brotherhood, supports Palestinian suicide bombings against Israeli targets and "consider[s] this type of martyrdom operation as an evidence of God's justice." Additionally, he encourages suicide bombers with statements such as, "Allah Almighty is just; through his infinite wisdom he has given the weak a weapon the strong do not have, and that is their ability to turn their bodies into bombs as Palestinians do."[5]

Shortly after the 9/11 attacks, I read excerpts from the diary of an imam who went on to be a suicide bomber. In his diary, he explains martyrdom is what all good, faithful Muslims should do because:

> We cannot live in the same world with the West. Western democracies have created a world in which we cannot exist, because in our world, the only thing to which we look forward to is the afterlife. This is just a temporary status, and we are moving on to something greater, and if we allow democracies, Western civilization, to survive, it will essentially turn the heads of all of our people and turn their heads away from the joys of the afterlife and the joys of this life. Therefore, we have to set ourselves on a path of destroying Western civilization.

To this many millions of Muslims are committed. Palestinian religious leader Suliman Satari expressed it even more directly on Palestinian television when he said in November 2005, "Destroy the infidels and polytheists! Your [Allah's] enemies are the enemies of their religion . . . ! Count them and kill them to the last one, and don't leave even one."

While these quotes are from Muslim clerics with speculative ties to terrorist groups, little is more frightening than listening to the beliefs and wishes of terrorist leaders. In February 2005, Hezbollah leader Sheik Hassan Nasrallah addressed 150,000 supporters in Beirut and vowed that the United States would suffer greatly as a result of its involvement in Iraq. "In the past, when the marines were in Beirut, we screamed, 'Death to America!' Today, when the region is being filled with hundreds of thousands of American soldiers, 'Death to America' was, is, and will stay our slogan," Nasrallah asserted. "The people of the region will receive [America] with rifles, blood, arms, martyrdom, and martyrdom operations."[6]

Hezbollah is considered as dangerous as al Qaeda. Responsible for the 1983 bombing of the U.S. Embassy in Beirut and the 1996 bombing of the Khobar Towers in Saudi Arabia, there is little doubt that their "Death to America" mission includes future operations on our own soil.

Since 9/11, al Qaeda has released numerous video and audio recordings promising attacks on the United States that would dwarf those on the World Trade Center and the Pentagon. "We announce that there will be new attacks inside and outside which would make America forget the attacks of September 11," claimed al Qaeda spokesman Abu Abdel-Rahman Al-Najdi.[7]

In a videotape released August 4, 2005, Ayman al-Zawahiri, al Qaeda's second in command, warned the United States: "If you continue your politics against Muslims, you will see, God willing, such horror that you will forget the horrors of Vietnam."[8]

Then, in January 2006, Osama bin Laden warned that "the nights and days will not pass without us taking vengeance like on September 11, God permitting. Your minds will be troubled and your lives embittered. As for us, we have nothing to lose. A swimmer in the ocean does not fear the rain." He concluded with the assertion that modern weaponry was no match for terrorists: "Don't let your modern strengths and arms fool you. They win a few battles but lose the war. Patience and steadfastness are much better. We were patient in fighting the Soviet Union with simple weapons for ten years, and we bled their economy and now they are nothing."[9]

Although I hope with all my heart that President Bush is right when he says that all men and women seek Western-style values, a close analysis of Eastern thought contradicts this view. As Huntington points out:

> Western concepts differ fundamentally from those prevalent in other civilizations. Western ideas of individualism, liberalism, constitutionalism, human rights, equality, liberty, the rule of law, democracy, free markets, the separation of church and state, often have little resonance in Islamic, Confucian, Japanese, Hindu, Buddhist, or Orthodox cultures. Western efforts to propagate such ideas produce instead a reaction against human rights imperialism and a reaffirmation of indigenous values.[10]

There are, however, glimmers of hope. I have become acquainted with members of the Iranian Diaspora living in the United States who are committed to the overthrow of the theocratic government in Iran. They appear to be devoted to a democratic, secular Iran, and they also consider themselves to be good Muslims. I have also met with imams and other leaders within the American Muslim community whom I believe to be sincere in their protestations of allegiance to both their faith and to the concept of religious diversity in the United States. On a broader stage, Arab countries such as Morocco, Dubai, and Qatar appear to be moving toward a more modern concept of the relationship between Islam and the state.

Will this become the norm throughout the Muslim world? Perhaps more important, will the modernization of Islam be the antidote to radical Islamic terrorists? Time will only tell. I do not, however, believe we can sit back, observe the tide coming in, and hope it is not a tsunami.

AMERICA AS THE LAST BASTION OF WESTERN CIVILIZATION

ACCORDING TO the Council on American-Islamic Relations (CAIR), there are more than seven million Muslims in the United States who have built more than two hundred mosques, schools, and community centers. They also claim to be one of the fastest growing religions in this country and around the world.

During a recent visit to the Detroit area, where there are at least sixty mosques and 130,000 Muslims, I was struck by how little assimilation has occurred. Dearborn had the look of a spruced-up Islamabad. While we stood on a street corner, we listened as the call to prayer went out over loud speakers on minarets all over the city. Every sign on every building was written in Arabic. Of course, this cultural isolation of the Islamic community is typical of all early immigrant communities in the United States. One would not be so concerned if the pressure from American society to assimilate *and* the desire of Islamic immigrants to do so were as strong today as those pressures and desires were in the past.

But the cult of multiculturalism has banned assimilation because that means there is dominance of one culture over another. The cultists have decreed that any expression of pride in things Western is forbidden

73

and any manifestation of concern regarding the threat posed by Islamification of society be punished. For instance, when several others and I objected to a memorial for the passengers of United Airlines Flight 93—the hijacked airliner that crashed in a field in western Pennsylvania on September 11—because it was shaped like a crescent, the media had a field day. Newspaper after newspaper devoted huge amounts of ink to lambasting me.

MEMORIAL TO TERROR

ON SEPTEMBER 7, 2005, just four days before the fourth anniversary of the 9/11 attacks, officials unveiled the winning entry for a memorial to Flight 93. It was called the "Crescent of Embrace"—an array of red maple trees symbolizing the Red Crescent of Islam in the way the cross universally symbolizes Christianity.

The design was created by Paul Murdoch of Los Angeles. He explained: "A crescent is part of the architectural vocabulary. It's a generic form used in design. We don't see any one group having ownership of it. You can call it all kinds of things. We can call it an arc. We can call it a circle. We can call it the edge of the bowl. The label doesn't matter to us in terms of intent."[11]

To me, it was completely unacceptable that any memorial to those who died in the 9/11 attacks would make even an oblique reference to Islam, considering that the hijackers who carried out the attacks were Muslim fundamentalists. "I don't know this country anymore,"[12] said one pundit, echoing my thoughts.

Author and syndicated columnist Michelle Malkin observed:

> I'm not an architect, but here is my 9/11 architectural philosophy: War memorials should memorialize war. If you want peace and understanding and healing and good will toward all, go build Kabbalah centers. Please, for the sake of those who have sacrificed, let's put the design of war memorials in the hands of creative people committed to erecting monuments of courage over capitulation. . . . A proper war memorial stirs one to anger and action. We all remember passenger Todd Beamer's last heard words as he and his fellow

Americans prepared to take back the plane from al-Qaeda's killers, don't we? No, the phrase wasn't, "Let's mediate." It was, "Let's roll!"[13]

Opposing the proposed design, I sent a letter to Fran Mainella, director of the National Park Service, a division of the Interior Department, which was in charge of approving any design. I argued that the crescent "raised questions . . . about whether the design . . . will in fact make the memorial a tribute to the hijackers rather than the victims whose mission the flight's passengers helped thwart." Given the sensitive nature of the memorial and its overall purpose, it seemed to me that the Interior Department should have directed the memorial design selection committee to choose a different design. "Regardless of whether or not the invocation of a Muslim symbol by the memorial designer was intentional or not," I wrote, "it seems that such a symbol is unsuitable for paying appropriate tribute to the heroes of Flight 93 or the ensuing American struggle against radical Islam that their last historic act and the 'Let's Roll' effort has come to symbolize."

The usual suspects were sympathetic to the design and the designer, accusing me of making a mountain out of a molehill and insisting that the design stand as is. Ibrahim Hooper, a national spokesman for CAIR (a group that regularly serves as chief apologist for radical Islam), accused me of having an "allergy" to their faith.

There were a few brave souls who made their support of my position known. "Have we gone so far down the dark and dingy PC road that we now honor those who kill us and have vowed to destroy our citizens and our country?"[14] columnist Sher Zieve wrote. "Allowing anything associated with terrorism to memorialize those heroic victims desecrates the final resting place of ground hallowed by their victory," added DiMitri Vassilaros of the *Pittsburgh Tribune-Review.* "Don't ask what the Flight 93 Advisory Commission was thinking when it chose this design from more than 1,000 entries. Obviously the members were not thinking. These airheads probably recommended planting Japanese cherry trees overlooking our sunken ships as the ideal memorial for Pearl Harbor."[15]

Tom Burnett Sr., whose son died in the crash, made an impassioned plea to his fellow selection-committee jurors about what he felt the crescent represented. "I explained this goes back centuries as an old-time

Islamic symbol," he said. "I told them we'd be a laughingstock if we did this." But instead of heeding his warning, he was ignored by the other panelists. As it turns out, "The jurors in their final report suggested the name of Murdoch's design be changed from crescent to something with less religious significance, like an arc or circle."[16]

The ensuing firestorms eventually forced the National Park Service to step in and change both the name of the memorial and the crescent of maple trees. I am sure Murdoch never contemplated a memorial design that could have been interpreted as a Christian symbol. If he had, the cult would have crucified him.

WHAT SHALL WE DO?

THE QUESTION arises, If we are indeed engaged in such an enormous struggle, what is required in order to be successful? Far beyond the obvious requirements of a well-equipped and well-trained armed force, we need to understand the nature of the conflict. We need to know exactly, as Sun Tzu admonished, who our enemy is and what motivates him. We must also know who *we* are. What places us in mortal danger is a lack of that knowledge. We apparently know little about our enemy while we, at the same time, struggle with an identity crisis of our own, which has been brought on by decades of politically correct propaganda being spewed out by the cult of multiculturalism. The problem is exacerbated by the massive infusion of millions of immigrants who come here without any desire to leave behind their old allegiances. And they are encouraged by the cult to avoid assimilation into what is left of the last bastion of Western civilization, a unique concept called America.

Congress appropriated more than $400 billion for the Department of Defense last year. Most of it went for the support of a traditional military infrastructure—guns and troops. These people are then organized into an army, navy, or air force. Yet our most dangerous enemy, with the possible exception of China, does not organize itself in the same way. It does not spend money on weapons systems, ships, or planes. It utilizes suicide bombers and inexpensive equipment: improvised explosive devices (IEDs), anthrax, and even suitcase nuclear devices. Just like the Kamikazes of World War II, our enemy's death is an indicator of his success. Today's enemy does not need a plane, although, as we have seen, they can be acquired temporarily. Our enemy does not need to be part of a national military force, nor does he need to follow orders from anyone empowered by a secular authority.

This phenomenon has rendered much of our war plans and strategies ineffective. When the fuel for a suicide bomber is religion, there is no technological gizmo that can defeat him. It is impossible to create a sensor to ferret out the individual who sees death as the doorway to a world of endless sensual pleasure. Additionally, the enemy knows that soon after he blows himself and his victims to bits, his mother will be giving thanks to God that her son is dead and that he has brought the world one day closer to the total Islamic victory promised in the Koran. And she will be receiving Saudi cash for her son's mission.

All this is perplexing for the cult of multiculturalism. It creates an impossible conflict of conscience. The cult's worldview is based on the immutable truth that no religion, culture, or country is less worthy of our respect than any other, unless, of course, it is part of Western civilization. They force themselves to rationalize the behavior of suicide bombers much like Bill Clinton and the NEA did after 9/11: by blaming America and the West for evoking such atrocities. According to the cult, we are under attack because we are wealthy . . . because we support Israel . . . because our forefathers were slaveholders . . . because of the Crusades . . . because we are mostly white . . . because too many of us still cling to Christianity . . . because we export *Baywatch* . . . because the image of the Prophet was used by a Danish cartoonist.

Of course, there is another reason why the cult is reluctant to articulate any opposition to Islamofascism: the cult has the same enemy— America. Islamic radicals view America as the "Great Satan," as Osama bin Laden describes us. We are the last obstacle to achieving spiritual nirvana on earth. The cultists, much like the terrorists, see us as the biggest impediment to a world cleansed of economic winners and losers and one in which our greatest allegiance will be to our humanness—not to a nation state.

Where do we go from here? If traditional forms of defense against aggression will not work, and many throughout the Western world cannot bring themselves to condemn the evil of Islamofascism, how can we survive? First, by coming to grips with who the enemy is. Then, by thinking long and hard about who we are. We as a society have to believe that what we have is worth saving and worth the long, hard struggle ahead of us.

Not long ago, a radio talk-show host asked me what America's response should be to a nuclear attack by Islamic terrorists. Of course, I said, our first option should be to think of something that would deter such an event. One option might be to threaten retaliation for such an attack by "taking out their holy sites." Nothing I have ever said evoked the kind of reaction that followed—and this time, the reaction was worldwide.

The death threats were numerous and serious. One report from a "credible source" had two teams of assassins dispatched from Pakistan to kill me. The cult of multiculturalism reveled in its near-universal condemnation of the mere suggestion that the West might ponder putting such a possibility on the table. But not all the reactions were negative.

Islamic scholar Robert Spencer originally disagreed with the thesis that such a threat would be a deterrent. But after witnessing the response to my hypothetical suggestion, he reconsidered. Interestingly, I received scores of supportive letters and e-mails from Scandinavians and even a few from Great Britain. One of the most interesting letters I received was from Beowulf Pels, author of the book *Edge of God*. His startlingly commonsense observation that, at the present time, there are no negative consequences to the action of a suicide murderer hit home. Instead, those who matter most to the murderers meet these actions with praise and adulation. Let me say now that if the threat of destruction of the religious sites would not deter the religious zealots, then we had better think of something that will. If all we do is kill the ones we can identify before they can commit their heinous deeds, we can expect the four horsemen of the apocalypse to be saddling up soon.

6

The Barbarians Are Past the Gate

It is the common failing of mankind never to anticipate the storm when the sea is calm.

—Niccolò Machiavelli

TESTIFYING BEFORE CONGRESS IN 2005, FBI director Robert Mueller Jr. revealed that his agency had "received reports that individuals from countries with known al Qaeda connections have attempted to enter the United States illegally using alien smuggling rings and assuming Hispanic appearances."[1] Mueller confirmed that the FBI suspected many of these people had changed their Islamic surnames and had adopted false Hispanic identities in order to escape detection and blend into American society.

Additionally, Richard Clark, the counterterrorism czar who worked in both the Clinton and Bush administrations, disclosed, "Of the 17,000 people who are missing in the United States somewhere, some are from countries of concern, and could be known terrorists. We really have no way of knowing who they are."[2]

After the September 11, 2001 attacks, U.S. Border Patrol agents experienced an increase in apprehending so-called special-interest aliens (SIAs) trying to sneak into this country from nations that we know support or tolerate terrorism. In 2003, the Border Patrol snagged about

39,000 illegal immigrants from countries "other than Mexico" (OTM), which includes SIA nations. By the end of 2005, that number had grown to 155,000, more than double the 76,000 apprehended in 2004.[3]

Evidence of terrorists in our midst does not stop there. U.S. and Mexican authorities are well aware of suspected training camps, one of them near Matamoros, Mexico, a few miles across the Rio Grande and south of Brownsville, Texas. There are reports that a large number of people are being trained in paramilitary warfare and exotic explosives in these camps, which are operated by the Zetas, a group of former Mexican military special forces troops who deserted in the mid-1990s to work as highly effective enforcers for the drug cartels. The FBI believes that such paramilitary organizations working in partnership with the drug cartels have the networks and the capacity to smuggle terrorists and weapons into the United States as easily as they smuggle drugs and people seeking jobs. Texas and federal law-enforcement agencies believe these paramilitary forces have been monitoring and evaluating U.S. law-enforcement operations along the Rio Grande.[4]

What raises suspicions even more among law-enforcement officials is that the training camps are frequented by a variety of ethnic groups, including Arab and Asian nationals. Since 9/11, Mexican authorities have reportedly apprehended hundreds of individuals with suspected terrorist ties in the border region. Sometimes the suspected terrorists are held in Mexico, and sometimes they are turned over to local U.S. authorities because federal officials will not accept custody. Most local law-enforcement agencies eventually turn them over to the FBI, but they never hear what happens to them.

Evidence of terrorist infiltration has led one retired federal agent—who is too nervous to talk about it publicly—to speculate that, for years, terrorists have been exploiting our porous Mexican and Canadian borders to bring explosives into this country. The former agent says he believes the explosives are designed to be detonated simultaneously in all parts of the United States.

In March 2006, FBI director Robert Mueller Jr. told a House appropriations subcommittee hearing that the FBI had broken up a smuggling ring organized by the terrorist group Hezbollah that had operatives cross the Mexican border to carry out possible terrorist attacks inside the United States. "This was an occasion in which Hezbollah operatives were assisting others with some association with Hezbollah in coming to the United States," Mueller told the subcommittee. He also testified that the organization had been "dismantled" and the FBI had identified the individuals who had been smuggled into the country.

Two things are striking about this latest FBI admission. First, we only learned of this event as an item in the FBI's annual report to the House appropriations subcommittee that controls funding for the bureau. The FBI did not inform the Congress or the American public about Hezbollah's activities in Mexico at the time they were uncovered and disrupted. No public announcement was made by the FBI. Instead, the news was buried in routine testimony. The second interesting facet of this statement is that it was not considered "newsworthy" by the mainline news media, so most Americans are still unaware that there are active Hezbollah cells in Mexico within a day's drive of our porous border.

MS-13, THE ZETAS, AND THE UNKNOWN

As my colleague and friend Charles Heatherly and I sat in a booth in a hotel restaurant waiting to meet with an informant, we wondered about the information he was bringing us. It turned out to be everything we could have hoped for. I cannot say much more about him. Suffice it to say, he was a former law-enforcement officer who wanted someone to know what he had come across in the years he had spent in the profession.

He began by telling us about Mara Salvatrucha, or MS-13 as it is commonly referred to. At that time, few had ever heard the name. That has since changed. The FBI has set up a unit devoted solely to this criminal gang.

Mara Salvatrucha is one of the most violent and bloodthirsty gangs ever to prey on our society. Originating in Los Angeles in the 1980s, the gang was founded by Salvadorans fleeing a civil war. The displaced Salvadorans found themselves settling in the poorest neighborhoods, unemployed, and disliked by other Hispanics. Its original members came from the leftist insurgent forces that opposed the Salvadoran government in the 1980s. Members were trained in firearms, explosives, and booby traps.[5] Considered one of the fastest growing gangs in the United States, MS-13 not only has a large presence in Los Angeles but also in Canada, El Salvador, Guatemala, Honduras, Mexico, and more than thirty U.S. states.

Most of MS-13's tens of thousands of members in the United States are illegal aliens. They are a huge problem in northern Virginia, where their calling cards are dismembered limbs that were severed by machetes. MS-13 is heavily involved in drug trafficking, human trafficking, assaults, homicide, robbery, extortion, turf battles, drive-by shootings, and exporting stolen cars to El Salvador. Additionally, MS-13 maintains links to other gangs in El Salvador, Guatemala, and Honduras.

Tattoos indicate both gang membership and one's area of responsibility. For instance, a dragon tattoo indicates the individual is involved in smuggling immigrants into the country. These *dragones* transport their human cargo from El Salvador through Mexico by train. Conductors and railroad officials are bribed to facilitate the mission. At some point, the cargo is transferred to vehicles to better penetrate the U.S. border. The routes are spotted with safe houses along the route to ensure their success. And make no mistake, they are highly successful in delivering their cargo.

Numerous media reports have featured intelligence officials' warnings of a connection between MS-13 and al Qaeda. In July 2004, reports surfaced of an al Qaeda figure meeting with MS-13 in Honduras in order to secure entry routes into the United States. Reports also surfaced that, during the summer of 2004, Iraqi Shi'ite cleric Muqtada al-Sadr was possibly in contact with MS-13 and/or the Farabundo Matri National Liberation Front (FMNL) in an attempt to get them to commit terrorist acts in El Salvador with the hope of forcing that government to withdraw its support for U.S. efforts in Iraq. The FBI will not comment on these reports.

Our informant also told us about the corruption that is spreading throughout the United States that is linked to Mexican-based drug cartels and the Mexican mafia. To interested observers within the law-enforcement community, there seems to be a pattern of corruption in which these cartels are buying influence and seeking comfort within U.S. cities. Like so many stories involving illegal immigration and drug smuggling, this story begins in Southern California.

The Tijuana-based Felix drug cartel and the Juarez-based Fuentes cartel began buying legitimate businesses in small towns in Los Angeles County in the early 1990s. They purchased restaurants, used-car lots, auto-body shops, and other small businesses. One of their purposes was to use these businesses for money-laundering operations. Once established in their community, these cartel-financed business owners ran for city council and other local offices. Over time they were able to buy votes and influence in an effort to take over the management of the town. They wanted to create a comfort zone from which they could operate without interference from local law enforcement.

In the small suburban city of Bell Gardens in central L.A. County, there was an effort to shut down the police department. City officials who would not cooperate with the Mexican-born city manager were forced out of office. Eventually, the L.A. County attorney's office moved in, and the city manager was prosecuted on charges of corruption. Unfortunately, Bell Gardens was only the tip of the iceberg. Other Los Angeles suburbs—including Huntington Park, Lynwood, and Southgate—became targets for the cartels.

The corruption spreading from south of the border is not confined to Southern California. In Cameron County, Texas, the former sheriff and several other officials were recently convicted of receiving drug-smuggling bribes. In Douglas, Arizona—where the international border runs down the middle of the town and divides it from its sister city of Agua Prieta, Mexico—the mayor's brother was discovered to have a tunnel from one of his rental properties going into Mexico.

The sad story of drugs and our porous borders doesn't end here, because no discussion of the problem is complete without recounting the story of the Tohono O'odham Indian Reservation in Arizona, which shares just a tiny fraction—seventy-one miles—of the nearly two-thousand-mile U.S. border with Mexico. Homes burglarized by illegals, deadly car wrecks caused by reckless smugglers, drug runners brandishing weapons as they demand help from the local people—all of this happens daily on the reservation. The reservation is the scene of one of the major drug corridors between the United States and Mexico. In 2002, tribal police seized 65,000 pounds of narcotics. During the first four months of 2003, tribal police reported seizing 33,000 pounds of marijuana and discovered 1,877 vehicles abandoned by smugglers. One of the busiest smuggling routes through the reservation begins about twenty-five miles to the west, where taxis finish a fifteen-minute run from Sonoyta, Mexico, by dropping off their passengers at a flimsy border fence.

Tohono O'odham children are being taken into the drug cartels, sometimes forcibly but oftentimes joining in for the money. On a visit to the reservation, I saw five-year-old children stumbling around stoned. Their parents are going crazy; they don't know what to do. They can't deal with the fact that they have been invaded.

THE WAR ON TERROR COMES TO OUR BACKYARD

SHERIFF SIGIFREDO Gonzalez Jr. of Zapata County, Texas, sees the sixty miles of border his deputies patrol as a front line in the war on terror. He says the biggest fear they face is that smugglers will bring terrorists and dirty bombs into the country through his county.

In November 2005, he told a conference in San Antonio that it was not a matter of if, but when a terrorist will enter the United States through Mexico with a dirty bomb or some other portable weapon of mass destruction. "We tried everything we know, with little success, to make the federal government aware of the problems we face and how they have affected us. The creation of the Department of Homeland Security has done nothing to help us," he concluded.[6]

Gonzalez has given credit to federal officials, however, for warning him that al Qaeda terrorists were looking to use smugglers, including the brutal MS-13 gang, to bring terror operatives across the border. "If smugglers can bring a hundred people or 2,000 pounds of marijuana into the United States, how simple would it be to bring terrorists into this country, or a suitcase loaded with a dirty bomb? I am very surprised it hasn't happened," he told a newspaper.

Gonzalez's frustration over the lack of cooperation from the Border Patrol was evident when Zapata County deputies responded to a rancher's report of people in black attire crossing his land late one night. The sheriff's department knew the rancher to be a solid, stable sort who would not concoct such a story, so deputies took up position on his land and waited. Around 9:00 p.m. one night they heard the footsteps of people marching in cadence. With the aid of night-vision equipment, they saw a group of approximately thirty men dressed in black and marching in twos. The first two men and the last two carried automatic weapons while the rest lugged large duffel bags between them. Since the deputies were outnumbered and outgunned, they quietly observed. As soon as they could, they reported to the sheriff in an attempt to get assistance from the Border Patrol. When the armed group moved toward a light in the distance near a paved road, the deputies withdrew.

Later, the sheriff learned that nineteen of the men had been apprehended. When he asked about their disposition, he was stunned to learn that they had almost immediately been returned to Mexico. Even worse, after reviewing pictures taken of the nineteen men, it was determined that one of them was one of the original thirty-one Zetas. Los Zetas is known for its heavy weaponry—AK-47 and AR-15 assault rifles—and its ties to drug trafficking, assassinations, kidnappings, and murders throughout Mexico. Follow-up inquiries yielded nothing. One can only speculate if corrupt officials, who are so pervasive on the border, were responsible for the return of these people to Mexico.

Other border authorities have filed reports of similar groups. In Jim Hogg County, Texas, Sheriff Erasmo Alarcon Jr., in a letter published in the local newspaper in the spring of 2003, warned of unidentified armed men dressed in military fatigues who had been spotted a number of times by area citizens and ranchers. The sheriff said that witnesses had described the men as wearing "professional-looking" backpacks and walking in military cadence.

In another Tex-Mex border county, a sheriff's department said deputies discovered a large metal container that had washed ashore from the Rio Grande. The container held several cylinders, each filled with papers covered with Arabic writing. This finding, among other evidence, is part of the reason why another Texas sheriff has prepared a training CD for the Border Patrol and other officers and agents working in the area. The CD features a picture of Osama bin Laden and urges officers and agents "to stop looking for him and start looking at the mega-drug cartels running rampant south of the border."

TERRORISTS AMONG US

IN DECEMBER 2005, the Department of Homeland Security sent word that authorities had arrested dozens of terrorist operatives who were already inside the country. While the total number of suspects was unknown, officials reported at least fifty-one people from countries known to support terrorist activities or harbor terrorist sympathies— Egypt, Iran, Iraq, Lebanon, Pakistan, and Syria—had been intercepted by the Border Patrol and other members of the Joint Terrorism Task Force (JTTF) since the unit began tracking such arrests a little more than a year before. These suspected illegal-alien terrorists had been apprehended for a wide variety of charges, including weapons smuggling and illegally wiring large sums of money into the country.

Though I had sought the information for some time, the December 2005 JTTF report was the first I'd seen that provided hard figures regarding suspected terrorists arrested inside the United States. It served as an admission of sorts by the government that there *is* a problem with terrorist infiltration. Prior to the report's release, much of the evidence had been anecdotal.

In August 2005, a Rand Corporation analysis stated that the United States was likely to be the next country that would experience suicide bombings similar to those carried out in London against mass-transit targets the month before. At about the time this report was released, federal, state, and local officials, along with a number of U.S. civilians, were discovering additional evidence of a terrorist presence in the country. Items such as discarded beverage boxes with Arabic writing, a jacket with a patch depicting an airliner flying into a tall building followed by the words "Midnight Mission," and other clothing, including an Arab military patch, proved this possible terrorist presence.

In November 2005, Texas congressman John Culberson released information that an Iraqi with ties to al Qaeda and on the terrorist watch list had been arrested and detained at the border. This apprehension, of course, fueled concern from several elected officials. "Remember that for every illegal border crosser caught at least another three make it in," argued Arizona congressman J. D. Hayworth. "We are playing a dangerous game of Russian roulette, and the longer we resist securing our border and enforcing our immigration laws, the more likely a terrorist incident becomes."[7]

If this incident isn't a wake-up call, I don't know what is. What scares me is not that list from federal law enforcement—after all, we've already caught those terrorists. What scares me is the potentially hundreds of terrorists who make their way through our porous borders each year and go undetected. Where are they? What are they planning? Where are they planning to strike? When? How many are there? How rough do the seas have to get before we know the storm is about to engulf us?

7

Autumn in Beslan

WHILE WE CAN ARGUE about the effects of immigration on our country, one thing is certain. We face something bigger than illegal aliens pouring over our borders. We and much of the civilized world face a foe whose face is pure evil. That evil manifested itself in a small community in Russia where a people, devoted to a cause and a set of ideas, decided that one of the best ways to advance their cause was to invade a school in a small town in Russia and take hostages: children, parents, and teachers.

For a few days in September 2004, I experienced what it would be like if terrorists personalized their attacks against Americans. I traveled to Beslan, Russia, in the immediate aftermath of an attack on a school by suspected Chechen Islamic militants. That anyone could be so ruthless to souls so innocent is as chilling as it is angering.

It was the evening of September 3, 2004, when I heard a radio news program report that gunfire and explosions had occurred at School Number One in Beslan, North Ossentia, Russia. I was driving home from my Denver office, a route that takes me within a block of Columbine High School. As the news continued, every horrible memory of my community's own day of terror came rushing back with a vengeance.

Two days earlier, about three dozen Islamic terrorists had stormed the Russian school, killed a few of its officials, and taken hostage nearly thirteen hundred children, ages seven to eighteen, as well as teachers and other personnel. There can be little doubt the terrorists timed their assault to coincide with Russia's annual "Day of Knowledge," a yearly observance at all schools during which children, dressed in their finest clothes and accompanied by their parents, participate in a number of education-related traditions. After a formal program of speeches from the staff and students, the first graders give a flower to the last graders. The last graders then take the first graders to their class, and so on.

Terrorists, acting under the guise of ideology, decided to seize the opportunity. All wore ski masks, and some wore explosive belts. In the takeover of the school, they exchanged gunfire with the police, killing five officers and losing one of their own. While security forces surrounded the school, shooting could be heard inside the buildings. The terrorists executed all the adult males—in front of the children—then tossed their bodies out of buildings later in the day. Video released by the terrorists showed the hostages herded into the gymnasium, where terrorists had strung explosives from the basketball hoops and positioned them over the children.

In negotiations with authorities, the Islamic terrorists threatened to kill fifty hostages for every one of their number who was killed and to kill twenty hostages for every one of theirs who would be injured. And if the building was stormed in a rescue attempt, the terrorists said they would set off the explosives.

For two days, Russian authorities tried negotiating with the terrorists, promising not to use force to free the hostages. On the second day, as the air became stifling inside the gym, the children shed some of their clothing. Some stripped down to their underwear. Some fainted from the heat. Others drank their own urine. As this horrendous event played out, one of the terrorists calmly sat among the frightened, cramped, miserable children and read his Koran.

The next day, the terrorists agreed to allow medical workers to remove the bodies still lying on the ground around the buildings. According to some reports, the removal team included agents of the Federal Security Service (FSB, formerly the KGB) who may have been recognized by the terrorists. As the team approached the compound, the terrorists opened fire and two explosions occurred in the gymnasium, creating a gaping hole. About thirty hostages tried to escape. But many of them were cut down in the crossfire between the terrorists behind them and the security personnel in front of them.

At that point, fearing the terrorists would kill the rest of the hostages, special forces troopers assaulted the school. The terrorists set off more explosions in the gym as panicked children and adults fled the smoke, fire, and chaos. Body parts were strewn all over. Witnesses reported seeing children gunned down. The heat from the explosives burned and singed other fleeing hostages. A terrorist dressed in a Russian army uniform yelled for the children to run toward him, then—after they surrounded him—he detonated the explosive belt he was wearing, killing himself and scores of them. After a two-hour gun battle, the security forces claimed to control most of the school.

In the end, the Russian government said "officially" 331 civilians and 11 soldiers had been killed and about 700 were injured. Thirty-one of the 32 attackers were confirmed dead; one had been captured. Of the civilian death toll, Moscow said that 156 were children, but this figure is disputed by the townspeople who know that the government routinely underreports casualties—as if 156 children are somehow better than losing 300, 400, or more.

After I learned of this tragedy, I knew I had to go to Russia as a show of compassion. My experience in the Columbine tragedy would allow me to help the people of Beslan begin to reconcile this horrible incident. My wife, Jackie—who taught Russian-language classes in Denver for twenty-seven years—and I had been to Russia nearly a dozen times with her students. We knew the country well. I was so pleased she was willing to go with me for what I knew would be a much different experience.

The morning after the Beslan horror, I contacted a local school district to see if it were possible to give American schoolchildren an opportunity to show their compassion for the Beslan students in some way. School officials seized on the idea, and the kids of Columbine High, as well as other schools in the district, responded beautifully.

The high school put up a twenty-foot-long poster in the school's cafeteria to sign and express their grief and condolences to the people and students of that distant Russian town. We met with the Columbine student leaders, many of whom were very eloquent in relating their wishes to bereaved people they didn't know half a world away. Younger middle-school and grade-school children, meanwhile, contributed more than a thousand handmade cards with personal messages.

SATURDAY AFTERNOON, SEPTEMBER 18, 2004

WE LANDED in Moscow. Those of us who had made previous trips to Russia were surprised by the significant changes in the city since the days of the Soviet Empire. Unlike that dreary past, today's Russian capital has a cosmopolitan air. It's a combination of Cleveland and Las Vegas. The new buildings have been designed to fit into the style of the older, beautiful buildings of the country's czarist past. Yet even the breathtaking changes in Moscow were not enough to erase the mental pictures imagined from the written accounts of the horror in Beslan. As we traveled from the airport to the American Embassy, the ambassador briefed me on political developments in the aftermath of the attack. The Beslan incident was only the most recent in a series of terrorist attacks throughout Russia and its former satellite states committed by Islamic militants and separatists. A month before, on August 24, 2004, suicide bombers brought down a pair of jetliners on domestic routes. Days later, on August 31, a Chechen suicide bomber killed nine people and wounded fifty more outside a crowded Moscow subway station.

Russian president Vladimir Putin, formerly head of the KGB for sixteen years during the Soviet era, used the events to roll back some democratic reforms, reinstating Stalinist measures and controls. He also fired some elected officials, appointing their replacements while proposing the elimination of political party selection of candidates for public office. Few voices of dissent remained, but they were a precious few—and their ranks thinned after each attack. In retrospect, it seems to me that the war against terror is now forcing the West to make similar choices. The ongoing debate over elements of the Patriot Act is our own iteration of this challenge.

SATURDAY NIGHT, SEPTEMBER 18, 2004

THE RUSSIAN press has interviewed us on national radio and television to discuss our trip here. Repeatedly we were forced to redirect the discussion to our *real* reason for being there: to deliver condolences and messages of hope from the American people, specifically, from the people of Columbine. But the interviews always gravitate back to President Bush's comments regarding Putin's reaction to the terrorist attacks. The United States is accused of practicing a double standard: criticizing Putin's hard-line approach while America aggressively pursues its own war on terror. The Russians, it seems, are not interested in making distinctions between Chechen rebels who happen to be Muslims and Osama bin Laden's jihad against America and the West. I agree there is a modicum of hypocrisy on our part; the threat is *militant Islam*. And it doesn't matter if it manifests itself in Beslan or New York City, or whether its practitioners are Chechen, Saudi Arabian, or from Oregon.

Even before we left the United States, we were having some trouble with the Russian foreign ministry. They didn't want us to go to Beslan, explaining that security might not be sufficient. While that may have been the case, it's never easy to know what's real and what's subterfuge in Russia. We understood that our presence made us tempting targets for terrorists, and I was apprehensive about that. But I also knew that the problems were not all related to security; the Russians were concerned about what we would see.

I was in contact with my friend Pastor Porter, who had been in Beslan for several days. He graciously offered transportation and accommodations in the compound of his church ministry—if we could make it that far. And we had trouble right up until the night before we were to leave. We were interviewed on an immensely popular Russian talk-radio program that covered most all of the country, including Beslan. We told the audience about the trouble we were having, and I explained the purpose of our trip and the Columbine connection. That approach had a much more positive effect than I imagined. The next morning, the foreign ministry withdrew its objections to our trip.

SUNDAY MORNING, SEPTEMBER 19, 2004

WE TRAVELED to the subway station to lay a wreath where an Islamic suicide bomber had earlier killed nine people. Plenty of cameras and media were on hand. And again I explained our purpose for being there. Finally, the questions became less hostile.

SUNDAY AFTERNOON, SEPTEMBER 19, 2004, HOSPITAL VISIT IN MOSCOW

OUR ENTOURAGE visited a pair of hospitals in Moscow where many of the young Beslan survivors were being treated. Room after room was filled with broken, battered, bloodied children, many with minds as damaged as their bodies. In every room there is a parent, aunt, brother, or grandparent keeping watch, nurturing the injured, lending a hand to change bandages, and otherwise tending their wounds.

We saw a severely injured sixteen-year-old boy lying quietly in his bed. He had the courage to grab one of the weapons dropped by a terrorist who had been shot, then he used it to shoot a terrorist who was firing on the children. Later, he threw himself over a small girl to protect her from a hail of bullets and flying shrapnel.

In another room, two sisters, ages eight and ten, were very quiet and somber. It was the eight-year-old's birthday, so Jackie sang "Happy Birthday" to her in Russian. Never having heard the song before, the little girl lit up the room with a smile. Her aunt, however, began to cry. She told me that her nieces had not yet been told that both of their parents had been killed in the attack. "They're smiling now," she said, "but it's because they do not know."

As we moved from room to room, it became more difficult to hear the stories of these children—stories of bravery, survival, horror, pain. We met the mother of a twelve-year-old girl who showed us a ball bearing that doctors had removed from her daughter's lung. The terrorists had laced their bombs with them, adding shrapnel to the blast effects.

Jackie went from child to child, chatting with them, comforting them as best she could, explaining who we were, why we were there, and offering the help we hoped to bring to all of them. We shared the experience of Columbine with them, telling them that the kids at the school had written the cards and letters we handed out. We told them that people all over the world were praying for them, and we prayed with them as well. I handed each injured child dozens of the cards and read many of them aloud because they were in English. Some of the wounded children were able to talk about their injuries, but others merely stared blankly at us or at the ceiling, still trying to sort through the awful trauma in their minds. When we arrived back at our hotel, Jackie and I were emotionally drained.

In the morning, I will be going to Beslan, but Jackie will be staying in Moscow. Today was hard, but I have no doubt that tomorrow will be even harder. We made four reservations on the next plane out—not an easy thing since there is only one daily flight to Beslan from Moscow on good ol' Air Siberia. The entourage is down to a U.S. Embassy representative, a navy control officer, a staffer from the House International Relations Committee, and me.

MONDAY MORNING, SEPTEMBER 20, 2004, HEADING TO BESLAN

GETTING TO the airport was unbelievably difficult. The traffic was like nothing I've ever seen in my life. The gridlock was in all directions for miles and miles. I didn't think we would make that one flight out, so I prayed silently, "Lord, if I am not meant to go on this trip, so be it. But if I am, please help me!" At that point, the driver of our car began driving on sidewalks, through parks, whatever he could go to get us to the airport. We made it on time. We should arrive in a few hours.

MONDAY AFTERNOON, SEPTEMBER 20, 2004, IN BESLAN

AS OUR plane landed, I saw armored U.N. vehicles on the tarmac; military personnel were everywhere. We were whisked to the school after brief introductions to city officials and local members of the Russian Duma (lower house of representatives). The sun was shining and the surrounding landscape enticing. All seemed tranquil—not at all like the scene of one of Russia's worst terrorist attacks. It was deceiving, especially knowing the area was still a tinderbox of ethnic hatred and political intrigue. Worse, after the massacre, the locals began to turn their rage toward their government for mishandling the incident. And of course, they harbor few good thoughts for the neighboring republics of Chechnya and Ingushetia, from where the terrorists came.

Arriving at the school—or what is left of it—we found thousands of water bottles and scraps of bread scattered about. These are memorials, we are told, to the children who were held for three days without food and water in the sweltering heat. As many as one hundred people were milling around the scene, not talking, just sobbing.

Townspeople gathered to catch a glimpse of us and figure out who we were. They followed us to the burned-out shell of the gym, where we placed a memorial wreath, a remembrance on behalf of the people of the United States. After a moment of silence, we put up the Columbine High School banner on a wall. It was a moment I will never forget. Local officials were visibly moved by the display of kinship and compassion from kids so far away who, unfortunately, could relate in some way to the horrible events that took place here. Somehow, when they saw the word "Columbine," I heard someone in the crowd pronounce it. They *knew* the word, what it meant, knew what had happened there. The school principal came to me, and together we shed a few tears.

Afterward, we were led around the building and shown where most of the children and parents died. The gym was only about forty feet by eighty feet. Into that small space the terrorists stuffed more than a thousand people for fifty-eight hours. From there we were shown where a cluster of terrorists had held out until three shells from a tank killed them. Then we were taken to a spot where two female terrorists blew themselves up as the shooting began. Our guides showed us the site where townspeople had captured one of the terrorists and beat him to death before hanging his body.

We learned the grim news that, although it had been more than two weeks, officials said that more than two hundred people were still unaccounted for. The townspeople believe the number is even higher. Many bodies still had not been identified.

We next visited the cemetery and saw six hundred newly dug graves. It was a disturbing sight when one pondered that it was nearly impossible to find a single person in the town of twenty-five thousand who was not touched, not affected in some personal way by so many deaths. We paused for another moment of silence and then left for the relative safety of the armored vehicles.

Russian security personnel were getting a little nervous about our being there. Their concern was not based on a wariness of another terrorist event, but rather they were worried about kidnappings. This threat plagues this region and happens hundreds of times a year. Security forces feared that the kidnapping gangs might exploit the situation.

On our way back to the airport, we discussed what we had just seen. It was doubtful we'd ever really know all the facts. But we did know that this unspeakable act of terror would leave generations of scars, both physical and mental. In this land of vendettas, the Beslan attack may serve as the impetus for future violence, future retribution.

As if to underscore the horror I had witnessed in Beslan, a news story a few weeks after I returned to the States reported that twenty-five suspected Chechen terrorists had entered the country from Mexico.[1] American intelligence officials said that they believed the Chechens had ties to Islamic militants in their home country—just like the thugs who slaughtered scores of men, women, and children in Beslan.

Many experts predict the next wave of terrorist attacks in the United States will be carried out against so-called soft targets—schools, office buildings, sports arenas, city streets—not necessarily in our largest cities. They are just as likely to take place, nearly simultaneously, in smaller cities, towns, and suburbs around the country. With this in mind, and given the fact that the terrorists have no qualms about killing children, what precautions are *not* appropriate? What is it, exactly, that we *shouldn't* do to protect ourselves?

So many innocent children in Beslan died horrible deaths because a group of terrorists decided to pursue a course they believed would advance their cause. But they did not achieve that goal. The civilized world reacted in horror and disdain and has tried to send the message to terrorists worldwide that those who perpetrated this crime did not convince anyone that their goal was worthy. The world instead saw the terrorists for what they are. They are evil.

As if the Beslan example weren't enough, al Qaeda spokesman Suleiman Abu Gheith asserted in an article published on the Alneda Web site in June 2002: "We have the right to kill four million Americans—two million of them children—and to exile twice as many and wound and cripple hundreds of thousands." In a separate communiqué found on a computer used by Osama bin Laden and other al Qaeda leaders (and containing an unfinished justification of the 9/11 attacks), U.S. officials found the essay "The Truth About the New Crusade: A Ruling on the Killing of Women and Children of the Non-Believers." Written by Ramzi bin al-Shibh, who worked with Khalid Sheikh Muhammad in organizing the 9/11 attacks, he argues that "the sanctity of women, children, and the elderly is not absolute" and concludes that " in killing Americans who are ordinarily off-limits, Muslims should not exceed four million noncombatants, or render more than ten million of them homeless."[2]

I would not advocate the suspension of habeas corpus or a declaration of martial law, but I would be among the last to complain about commonsense measures such as terrorist profiling, eliminating all immigration from terrorist-sponsoring nations, and securing our borders in order to allow the government to do all it can to protect and defend the country.

Evil prowls this planet. It searches for easy targets. And it strikes without mercy. It struck in Russia, and thousands of people today are grieving as a result. Some people will suggest that, although this was a horrible crime, the people who perpetrated this atrocity were provoked to act in this way because they had been ill treated by the past government in Russia. But I can conceive of nothing that could justify this assault in Beslan. No amount of rationalization, no amount of historical injustice can exonerate the horror inflicted on the people of that community.

While it is extremely painful to discuss things such as the Beslan incident, it is important that we do so. It is important that we try to understand what motivates terrorists to do what they did. And it is important that we decide in advance what we will do in response to such atrocities so that we will not fall victim to repetitions of the same kind of barbarism.

PART 2

Our Broken Immigration System

8

Our Porous Borders

By deterring the settlement of new illegals, by increasing deportations to the extent possible, and, most importantly, by increasing the number of illegals already here who give up and deport themselves, the United States can bring about an annual decrease of the illegal-alien population, rather than allowing it to continually increase.

—Mark Krikorian, May 2005

M ASS IMMIGRATION IS THE sole reason the U.S. population is nearing 300 million people.[1] It's why the U.S. Census Bureau estimates that, at current rates, the U.S. population will surpass 420 million by 2050.[2] As long as we continue to have porous borders, the problems associated with mass immigration—threat of terrorist infiltration, loss of American jobs and wage depreciation, urban sprawl and congestion, increased spending for social services and welfare benefits, soaring health-care costs, rising costs for incarceration, increased education costs with a resultant decrease in education quality—will all continue to get much worse and much more expensive for the American citizen-taxpayer.

To put the problem into perspective, in a single six-month period— from October 2003 to March 2004—some 500,000 people were able to pass through just *one sector* of our southern border at Tucson, Arizona. How do we know that many illegals passed through? During that same time, the Border Patrol apprehended about 250,000 illegals. And the Border Patrol estimates that at least two or three illegals get through for every one it apprehends. These are astronomical numbers, but given our country's poor record of border enforcement, they aren't surprising—just disappointing and alarming.

Enforcement measures have ranged from the well intended but ineffectual to the illogical and absurd. For example, Border Patrol agents have been assigned to sit at a specific point on the border and ordered by their supervisors not to move from that spot—not even if they see illegals trying to cross the border at some point down "the line." These agents were told that their *only purpose* was to intimidate, not halt, people from entering the country. That's not enforcing the law. That's mocking the law! My answer to the problem of border enforcement is simple: if we're not devoting enough resources to it, then devote *more* resources to it.

In the fall of 2005, the venerable CBS News program *60 Minutes* broadcast a segment on illegal immigration during which Ed Bradley interviewed me. He asked if I believed the United States was doing enough to protect our borders from a host of threats: illegal immigration, drug and weapons smuggling, possible terrorist infiltration. I replied that I didn't believe we were. I pointed out that we weren't spending nearly enough on border security. Bradley asked me how much I thought we should spend, and I answered quickly that we should be spending *billions* more than we are. It is Congress's duty to do whatever it takes to protect and defend our borders. If we can't stem the flow of millions of illegal aliens, how can we possibly hope to stop terrorists from infiltrating the country?

In my congressional district, the city of Aurora is approaching a population of five hundred thousand. Using the data mentioned at the beginning of this chapter, that means that at just one sector of our border with Mexico, our country adds another Aurora, Colorado, every six months.

In addition to all these illegal entrants—the total number of which is estimated to be in the millions every year—the United States *legally* takes in approximately 1.5 million immigrants annually, making us one of the most generous (read *liberal*) nations in the world in terms of immigration policy. That's a lot of people. At least when they come into the country legally, we know who they are, where they are, and why they're here.

Of course, we cannot say the same for illegal aliens. But we are told not to worry, because *most* of them pose no threat. We're told they are simply here "do the jobs that no one else wants to do." The White House, politicians, and corporations tell us that mass immigration is harmless because it provides an overall benefit to our country and its economy.

As a Republican in a GOP-controlled House, governing with a Republican-controlled Senate and led by a Republican president, I recognize that many times I rile my colleagues. I have certainly upset the White House because I talk about our porous borders as often as I can. I talk about the problem because I believe it is one of the most important public-policy issues with which we must deal.

Living in Washington DC; Chicago, Illinois; Billings, Montana; or Omaha, Nebraska, one can see some of the effects of illegal immigration. But one cannot truly get the whole picture until one views them at the border. Too few in government will admit it, but there are grave consequences to this kind of massive immigration—the kind of consequences too few in government want to discuss, even though American citizens are suffering every day for it.

I received a letter from Rhonda Rose in Arizona, and it certainly put a face on the issue of illegal immigration for me. It reminded me that there is a very human side to this problem on *our* side of the border, and that the problem is not just about numbers. When we talk about the fact that a quarter of a million people were interdicted in just one sector along the border during a span of six months, that is just a number to most people. But to Rhonda Rose and the thousands of people who live along our border with Mexico, where our immigration problem is the worst, it's about far more than just numbers. Their lives are interrupted and sometimes destroyed. She wrote:

> I live in a world where I do not count. I am not a minority. I am poor. I do not have coalitions rallying for what I feel is important. I do not have news reporters writing about poor me. But I have views, I vote, I pay taxes, and I know there are millions of people in America just like me. I live next to a shelter built by politicians who are afraid to have an opinion about closing the border. Daily,

1,500 illegal aliens visit that shelter. It was supposed to keep those poor people from urinating and defecating on the streets. It did not. Now, if I were to defecate on the streets, I would be fined.

My home and vehicles have been broken into twenty-two times in five years. I stopped calling the police each time they do now, because they do not come anyway. Instead, we bought a gun. We scared off the last illegal alien trying to steal our truck. He knew enough English to say "sorry" as we pointed the gun at him. Three months later, we still have a towel over the smashed driver's side window. Not too long ago a car ran into the rear end of my car. The policeman came and said I would have to wait while he called for backup. My baby was screaming. The police had no film in the camera. The backup policeman had no fingerprinting ink or film. The illegal alien who hit me had an ID, but the police said there was nothing that could be done. The illegal would just get another fake ID and would never show up for court. He did not have insurance. The illegal alien who hit me said "sorry" as he walked away. He was free to go. I was free to pay the deductible on my car repairs and the chiropractor bills for my children and myself. If I drove without insurance and hurt someone or their possessions, I would be forced to pay for the damages.

My husband works six days a week as a framing contractor. He pays FICA, Social Security, state taxes, Federal taxes, general liability insurance, workman's comp insurance, and probably others I do not even know about. His workman's comp just skyrocketed from $5,000 to $28,000 a year. Now, I ask you, where am I going to come up with the extra $23,000? We had no claims. Should I take it from my food budget? My home insurance costs me $100 more annually because I live in a border state. How long before Kansas becomes a border state?

I have no medical insurance and have had no medical insurance for years. I cannot afford it. At thirty-three, I got cancer. My doctor told me to go to the hospital. I do not remember how to spell the state's medical system, since they declined me anyway. My husband's company had no profits for six months due to theft. Without studying my receipts, I was declined. Interestingly, hundreds of illegal aliens standing in line were being given food stamps and medical care. They did not have Social Security numbers; they did not speak English.

My son cries nightly because his arms and legs hurt. He has cried for almost seven years. They do not know what is wrong with him.[3]

Rhonda and her husband were hesitant to take their son to a doctor because they had no health insurance and couldn't afford it. She went on to say, however, that when she has been forced to seek care at a local hospital emergency room, the staff doctor could not see them because there were so many illegals ahead of them. U.S. law forbids hospitals from turning away patients just because they can't pay for care, regardless if they are in the country illegally. As such, illegal aliens regularly abuse the law. Since hospitals can only see so many people before they are overwhelmed, many U.S. citizens are prevented from receiving the care they so desperately need. Rhonda continued:

Two years ago I announced to my family there would be no turkey for Thanksgiving. We would eat pasta and be thankful we are a family. My Catholic friend made arrangements for me to get a box of food from her church. I went reluctantly. I drove up in my broken old van. I saw a lot of new stickers on new Suburbans. My van was the worst vehicle there, and it hit that I was really poor.

I stood in line for twenty minutes, amazed by the number of illegal aliens who could not show an ID when they were asked. When it was my turn to show an ID, I was told to leave. There was not enough food for me to take a box. I looked around; there were boxes of food everywhere. For a minute I forgot: I did not count.

Our church, our pastor, reminds us to stay hopeful. I struggle to make sense of a system that has taken from me and given to those who have more than I do. Who will be my voice? Where is my coalition? I thought it was the leaders of America. I was wrong. They have sold me out, and millions like me. What is worse, I do not know why.[4]

Rhonda Rose's story is not unique. Another couple lived in Houston, Texas, for thirty-two years before finally deciding they'd had enough. They had grown weary of watching their community die a slow, painful death due to mass immigration. Houston, like much of the Southwest, had been slowly transformed from a uniquely American city into a multicultural wasteland where U.S. residents were giving way to a rush of illegal aliens. Worse, no one—not the local government, not the state government, and certainly not the federal government—seemed to care that one of the nation's largest cities was being diluted into an ethnically unrecognizable multicultural-opolis.

The woman, a faculty member of the department of psychology at the Baylor College of Medicine, and her husband, a native Texan from a small town near Abilene, described their plight this way:

> The large Latino population that arrived in Houston from Mexico, Guatemala, and El Salvador has not, in my opinion, made Houston a better or even a more interesting city. It has instead caused the same kind of blight, followed by white flight, that every other influx of poor, uneducated people has caused in other parts of the country. To whom does the good accrue from mass immigration into our cities? To the immigrants themselves, many of whom are rewarded for breaking the law after they enter illegally, and to those who benefit from cheap labor. But the very high price of so-called cheap labor is paid for by displaced U.S. citizens of every race, and it can be a high price indeed.
>
> Those of a liberal bent have recently discovered "sprawl," and they claim to be against it. Houston is one of the best examples of sprawl that anyone can find. In the 1950s Houston had a population of about 250,000. There were good public schools and very little crime. By the time we left in 1980, it was becoming increasingly congested and unsafe in the downtown. It took longer and longer to drive to work and come home.
>
> By 1980, much of Houston's Anglo population had begun the great escape from the city center to the suburbs. Ten years later, much of the professional and business classes were fleeing even farther west, away from the older suburbs and "into Ford Bend

County," where newer, self-sufficient subcities had been built. Still the problems worsened; even the ritzy residential areas were forced to hire private police to protect residents and property from frequent robberies and drive-by shootings.

Eventually the mass immigration of noncitizens—and the inherent cultural, crime, and economic problems they brought with them—forced tens of thousands of longtime Houstonites to make the decision to leave the area for good. Only by now, so much degradation and blight had been imported along with the immigrant masses, many residents could not sell their homes. Upscale communities were buttressed against one-time attractive apartment complexes that had declined into impoverished immigrant slums, some small apartments built for a family of four holding a family of ten or more. As a result, many of the owners simply abandoned their properties to a new group of slum landlords for a pittance. Repairs were rare, which led the area to degrade even further.

As poverty and blight increased, so did crime. Residents report the area became infested with drug trafficking and drug use. Police, it seemed, were nearly powerless to do much about it. They would stage shows of force, but they only lasted a few weeks; once the operations were over, the drug-dealing and lawlessness returned.

Day laborer sites sprang up—and much of the drug-dealing took place there—but even federal immigration officials were unable to intervene. Immigrant rights groups were hamstrung by allegations of rampant "civil rights" abuses.

A multicultural mix is only possible between people of similar education, occupation, and affluence. Without that social class similarity, self-segregation inevitably follows. If cosmopolitan implies being polished and civilized, I'll take the Houston of the 1950s.[5]

These Americans and millions of others are asking their government to stop ignoring them. They have pleaded with their leaders on the state and federal level to do *something* about illegal immigration. They are not asking us to slam shut the door on people, and they are not asking us to act out of racially motivated reasons or any of the other ugly aspects of the immigration debate. That is not what motivates people along the border. They are devoted to their land. They are devoted to their country. They believe in the rule of law, and they are simply asking that the law be enforced so they can have a life free of personal invasion.

What Americans must understand is that while we have always had illegal immigrants and illegal immigration, the dynamics of our border problems are changing—for the worse. Today, it is no longer a few people coming across the border looking for jobs. It is now a very well-organized effort conducted largely by people who have heretofore been involved with drug smuggling. Because people smuggling has become very lucrative, drug cartels have become more interested. They are paid between a thousand to fifteen hundred dollars to get a Mexican national into the United States; costs for a Middle Easterner or an Asian rise to about fifty thousand dollars.

Over the course of my legislative career I have tried to deal with the issue of immigration reform in a variety of contexts. I've talked about the problems associated with porous borders and what they mean to the future and security of the United States. I've talked about the economic impact of the massive immigration of low-skilled, low-wage workers. I've talked about the environmental damage.

By the year 2050, if we do absolutely nothing and things continue as they are today, the U.S. population will reach some 420 million people, with a vast majority coming from non-English-speaking nations.

The fact that we may reach that number via illegal immigration and the descendants of illegal immigrants may be a very good thing. It may be very positive for the United States to have population growth of this nature, which will be so dramatic and so important in terms of many things, including the economy. We talk about the need for growth in the economy, so maybe it is a good thing. But we have to make a decision as to whether or not this is the way we want to get to the year 2050, and whether mass immigration will be in our best interests.

I come from Colorado, and things have changed pretty dramatically in my state over the last several years. The increase in Colorado's population has already been substantial. As such, the infrastructure costs that go along with massive increases in people are, of course, prevalent, and the taxpayers of my state are paying them for.

But this kind of growth is happening across the country. Soon, if immigrant growth rates persist, it will be much more difficult to get through congested highways, to visit our national parks, to experience the pristine wilderness that we have all enjoyed, and to provide benefits for millions and millions of new arrivals. I can't begin to estimate what that will cost us.

The sheer number of immigrants is something far greater than anything we have ever experienced in this nation. It is far greater than what we experienced in the 1900s when my grandparents came here. But maybe it will all be worth it. Maybe giving all of that up is worth it because the economy demands this kind of population growth, right?

I am not saying that we should slam the door on all immigration. But what I am suggesting is it is important to review as a nation the effects of massive immigration and whether or not we feel the price is about right or if it is far too steep.

After I've spoken about our porous borders on the floor of the House—which I try to do as often as I can—the e-mails, telephone messages, and letters start all over again. There is such an outpouring of emotion from Americans on this issue. They, too, feel it is vital that we do something about our borders.

Most of the feedback comes from Americans who are watching their lives and livelihoods disrupted. They often ask the Congress to do *something* about this illegal immigration problem. Speaking for myself, I am overwhelmed by these cries for help. And I know my colleagues care about this issue. But I don't see that care being translated into any sort of help for these Americans who put up with this hellish nightmare day in and day out. The Congress appears fearful of doing anything that would actually secure our borders, fearful of doing anything that would actually enforce the law in this country. Why? The fear stems from political reasons, and that disappoints me.

Let me reiterate how important it is for immigrants to adopt their new life around a set of common ideals. I have to say this repeatedly in order to reemphasize that I am not opposed to immigration. But our immigration policies are in desperate need of reform.

In terms of physical security, there is so much we can do. We have the resources to erect a fence along the *entire* border—not just along our frontier with Mexico, but with Canada as well. High-tech, two-layer fences have been set up at some portions of the border, and they have been effective. What's more, the plan is cost-effective; we can build a border-length fence for about $1.5 million per mile: $3 billion for a two-thousand-plus-mile fence along our southwestern border. Given what we would save in terms of providing so many benefits for illegals, I have no doubt we could recoup this investment in no time. That $3 billion figure, by the way, is less than we're spending per month in Iraq.[6]

But I cannot pretend that a border-length fence will *completely* eliminate all illegal immigration. Still, a fence will go a *long* way toward accomplishing that goal. Remember, Border Patrol agents report that two to three illegals get past them for every one they apprehend—a figure that translates into fifteen thousand to twenty thousand *per day*. A fence would almost certainly reduce this ratio to something very manageable.

To bolster the physical protection of our borders, the president should also deploy U.S. military troops, when feasible, to support the Border Patrol. To facilitate that, we should amend the criminal statute of posse comitatus, which some believe bars the use of military in a border-enforcement capacity. This *works*. In April 2005, 444 soldiers in the U.S. Army's 4th Squadron, 14th Cavalry Regiment of the 172nd Stryker Brigade conducted desertlike training in conjunction with the Border Patrol in New Mexico. They were responsible for aiding federal agents in the apprehension of more than 2,500 illegal aliens and 6,900 pounds of marijuana. By all measures, officials reported that Operation Bootheel was a success.[7]

We have the necessary technology, combined with human resources, to secure our borders tomorrow. It is a canard for politicians to say it's impossible and that we must figure out a different way to defend America rather than defending our borders. What they are really saying is: I choose not to defend and secure our borders because there are political ramifications that I fear. It is those fears that put the life of every American citizen in mortal danger.

9

The Myths of Immigration

Tom Tancredo has done everyone a favor by stating plainly the immigration rejectionists' endgame—turn the United States into the world's largest gated community.

—*Wall Street Journal*, December 29, 2005

THE SEPTEMBER 20, 2004, *Time* magazine cover featured a pair of hands grabbing and ripping a hole in the red-and-white-striped portion of an American flag. The headline glared: SPECIAL INVESTIGATION, AMERICA'S BORDERS: EVEN AFTER 9/11, IT'S OUTRAGEOUSLY EASY TO SNEAK IN. Inside, a nine-thousand-word article titled "Who Left the Door Open?" laid bare a phenomenon that authors Donald L. Barlett and James B. Steele called "scandalously" obvious: illegal immigrants are overrunning ever-widening portions of our country, and in the process, they are making a mockery of our laws, bloating already strained state and local budgets, costing businesses millions of dollars, and endangering our national security.

If I didn't know better, I would have sworn *I* had written the piece. So much of what the writers "revealed" about the problems associated with illegal immigration has been the centerpiece of what I have been railing about for years.

The article began with a bit of irony. Barlett and Steele pointed out how, since 9/11, Americans have endured increased security screening

111

at airports. Our luggage is carefully checked, we're physically searched, our laptop computers and other electronic devices are scrutinized, we even have to remove our shoes—thanks to a certain would-be "shoe bomber" named Richard Reid—as part of this enhanced security. Yes, it's inconvenient, but most people don't mind, because they understand the new procedures are necessary and reasonable.

Meanwhile, at our border crossings, cars line up as agents work to improve the system of confirming the identity of incoming visitors as well as making sure that these people are not bringing weapons or drugs into the country. To accomplish this task, the government has provided Customs agents with the technology to help them do a better job of admitting the right people while keeping the wrong people out. Some people could say these improvements in security were a long time coming—and they'd be right—but the point is, the *Time* writers say, these things are being done now in the name of homeland security.

Contrast these rational measures with the distinct *lack* of security applied to our porous borders, the magazine concluded, and you wind up exposing a gaping hole in our national effort to, not only keep out those who seek to do us harm, but to deal with a problem—illegal immigration—that worsens with each passing day.

I couldn't agree more that since the 9/11 attacks, U.S. borders have actually grown even more porous. Based on *Time's* investigation, not Tom Tancredo's point of view, the number of illegal aliens flooding into the United States in 2006 will top three million. That is enough to fill twenty-two thousand Boeing 737-700 airliners, enough for sixty flights a day for a year.

Undoubtedly, *Time* made the open-borders crowd very uncomfortable. As I can attest, any time they are confronted with such plain-spoken and powerful truths about illegal immigration, they tend to circle the wagons and cover their ears. That's why it is so difficult to get to the truth about the problem of illegal immigration: too many people refuse to hear it, discuss, it, or acknowledge it, even though it is staring them in the face. This refusal to engage in an open, honest debate about the problem has also led to a number of falsehoods regarding the problem. And these falsehoods are now generally accepted as truth.

A December 2005 editorial in the *Wall Street Journal* was typical in its incorrect and tainted portrayal of the problem of mass immigration. In taking aim at a major piece of immigration reform legislation I helped guide through the House a few weeks earlier, the paper mostly mocked and ridiculed me rather than argue against my proposals on their merits (or lack thereof). Usually when people disagree with you and make that disagreement personal, it's because they don't have the facts on their side to make a responsible argument. And this is illustrative of how so many myths regarding illegal immigration have come to pass.

The fact is, the measures contained in the reform legislation the House passed in early December 2005 would, if adopted, severely curtail the numbers of people flowing uninhibited across our borders. Though the measures were still *less* than what I wanted, the overall bill was the best start at real immigration reform in more than ten years. It called for the construction of nearly seven hundred miles of a two-tiered security fence, for employers to be required to verify that their workers are either U.S. citizens or in the country legally, for cities to stop providing sanctuary for illegal aliens by prohibiting their police from inquiring about a suspect's immigration status, and for changing illegal immigration from a civil penalty to a misdemeanor.

In debunking these sensible reform measures, the *Wall Street Journal* resorted to many of the same "the sky is falling" arguments that are not only demonstrably false but sound more like talking points issued by the U.S. Chamber of Commerce:

> Tom Tancredo has done everyone a favor by stating plainly the immigration rejectionists' endgame—turn the United States into the world's largest gated community. The House took a step in that direction this month by passing another immigration "reform" bill heavy with border control and business harassment and light on anything that will work in the real world. For the past two decades, border enforcement has been the main focus of immigration policy; by any measure, the results are pitiful. . . . The legislation is aimed at placating a small but vocal constituency that wants the borders somehow sealed, come what may to the economy, American traditions of liberty or the Republican Party's relationship with

the increasingly important Latino vote. . . . Sponsors of the legislation, led by House Judiciary Chairman James Sensenbrenner and Homeland Security Chairman Peter King, don't stop at targeting good Samaritans. They're also forcing the business community to simultaneously create jobs and kill jobs. . . . This also smears the law-abiding aliens with the lawbreakers. If a bill with this anti-guest-worker provision ever became law, millions of otherwise well-behaved people who have become integral parts of thousands of U.S. communities would have every incentive to stay in the shadows lest they be deported. As a matter of law enforcement priorities if nothing else, this is crazy.[1]

A "crazy" piece of legislation containing little that will "work in the real world"? For those willing to listen to reason—and most Americans are—it's time to set the record straight.

As was stated in previous chapters, illegal immigration does very little to benefit our country. For those of you who desire to join me in the fight to secure our borders and our future, remember the following:

- Myth no. 1: There is nothing the United States can do to stop illegal immigration.
- Myth no. 2: Illegal immigrants take jobs Americans don't want.
- Myth no. 3: Illegal aliens are an economic plus for America.
- Myth no. 4: Only bigots object and oppose illegal immigration.

The fact remains, nowhere are the American people and their leaders more profoundly at odds than over the issue of immigration—legal and otherwise. The public has repeatedly demanded serious reform. And these demands have only increased since 9/11. Americans want an end to illegal immigration, and they have said they support a reduction of the number of legal immigrants coming into the country.

Perhaps the most significant example of this problem was the passage of Proposition 200 in Arizona in November 2004. A majority of Arizonans—nearly 56 percent—recognized that the federal government had left them high and dry regarding illegal immigration. The borders were undefended. Internal enforcement of immigration laws had become a joke. Social services were being depleted. Funding for hospitals and schools was drying up. The crimes being committed by illegal aliens, along with incarceration rates, were skyrocketing. In short, the costs of illegal immigration to Arizonans only increased.

As more people realized their state had become an illegal immigration cesspool and the primary funnel through which millions of people a year were coming across from Mexico, they became increasingly impatient. So they reacted with the passage of Proposition 200, a measure that was opposed by every member of the U.S. Congress from the Arizona delegation, both Republican and Democrat. (Proposition 200 denied state benefits to anyone illegally in the country and required residents to prove they were citizens before they were allowed to vote.)

Remarkably, these are pretty radical ideas in this day and age. They are ideas that everybody wanted to run away from. The establishment, especially, wanted to run away from them. The media came out against it. The proponents campaigning for the measure's passage were outspent two and a half to one by the opponents of the measure.

Ultimately, Proposition 200 passed, and the amazing thing to note is that fully 47 percent of those who voted for the amendment were Hispanic.

The impact these facts ultimately has on the immigration-reform debate, I cannot know. But I do know that they create a dilemma for elected officials, because they are the reflective will of a majority of the American people, and that will differs significantly from the will of their elected representatives and the elitists.

Many politicians have decided that they can address this issue by finessing it: agreeing theoretically with people when they are in a forum in which doing so would be to their political advantage. It's easy to agree that, yes, there is a problem with immigration and, yes, we should do something about it. Many politicians tend to believe they can evade the issue by mollifying a certain portion of their constituency while simultaneously doing things to attract these other, very powerful, very vocal groups pressing for open borders and a relaxation of border-law enforcement. I don't believe finessing this issue can last much longer. Eventually—and soon—politicians will have to face up to the fact that they will have to deal decisively with mass immigration's ill effects on their constituents—or pay the consequences. The days of talking out of both sides of one's mouths are over.

Now that the truth is out, let's see how many of those who claim to speak for America will embrace it, and more important, act upon it. In the meantime, I'll be impatiently waiting for them to join me.

10

System Breakdown

This is a scandal of immense proportions that has got to be brought out into the open in congressional hearings and straightened out.

—Rep. John Culberson (R-TX)

IN THE WAKE OF 9/11, the Congress and President Bush approved the creation of the Department of Homeland Security (DHS). Among other things, it was hoped that combining dozens of federal agencies into one agency—each responsible for some aspect of national security—would improve efficiency, cooperation, and the sharing of information. But problems persist.

One of the agencies swallowed up by DHS was the Immigration and Naturalization Service (INS), an agency long criticized as much for its inability to effectively manage the nation's immigration system as for inherent corruption. The INS was reformed into the U.S. Citizenship and Immigration Services (USCIS) and further into the U.S. Immigration and Customs Enforcement (ICE) Agency and the U.S. Customs and Border Protection (CBP). Collectively, USCIS became responsible for anything having to do with immigration in the United States, including naturalization, work permits, adjustment of status (moving from a temporary to permanent work status), extensions of visas, and immigrant sponsorships (business and family).

Some of INS's corruption became clear when, during this transition phase in the fall of 2002, the assistant director for INS investigations in New York City and a pair of FBI Joint Terrorism Task Force (JTTF) officials were placed on administrative leave when it was discovered that INS had recently given U.S. citizenship to a known terrorist under investigation by JTTF.[1] Officials said the unidentified Middle Eastern male appeared on terrorist watch lists and was a member of the Hezbollah terrorist organization. It is possible that, had the agency done its job, the man would never have become an American citizen. Despite a number of attempts by adjudicators handling the alleged terrorist's naturalization case, the New York INS and the FBI's offices reportedly never responded to requests to hand over the person's "alien file." This A-file included biographical and status information such as name, date of birth, alien number, country of birth, dates of all INS actions, and other pertinent investigative data. It was not clear why the requests for the A-file were repeatedly ignored or why the adjudicators proceeded with the naturalization process without viewing the file, but it's believed the system itself may be at fault. Too often, adjudicators are forced to meet naturalization "quotas"; job-performance ratings and cash bonuses were often dependent upon the number of naturalization approvals an INS employee processed.

Since its creation, this inherently bad system has seen little improvement. In fact, in many respects, the situation has only worsened. The corruption included bribery, espionage, the selling of so-called green cards (some for sexual favors), and undue influence by foreign governments—some of which are believed to sponsor terrorism. This huge, tangled web of lies and deceit permeates virtually every aspect of the immigration process.

Perhaps the most telling thing about USCIS today, in spite of 9/11 and in spite of the war on terror, is the fact that many officials in charge of the agency still view their primary task as "customer service." They don't see themselves as the keepers of the gate. They don't think of themselves as enforcers of the law. And they don't see themselves as protectors of national security.

There is a small contingent within the USCIS, however, that *does* perform a law-enforcement duty. In fact, the primary objective of this group (the "enforcers") is the enhancement of national security. As one might imagine, they don't fit in very well with the rest of the agency and its "Wal-Mart greeter" mentality.

Created by former USCIS director Eduardo Aguirre (who was appointed by President Bush as U.S. Ambassador to Spain on June 24, 2005), the enforcers' small office is in charge of internal-affairs investigations as well as security for personnel, installations, and information for USCIS. As long as Aguirre was in charge, the enforcers were allowed to perform their duties. But as soon as Aguirre was promised the Spain ambassadorship, he essentially stopped making decisions and just took up space until it was time for him to leave.

When that happened, the enforcers—who reported directly to the director—were isolated. And that was fine with those in the agency who wanted the enforcers to fail and did everything in their power to see that they *would* fail. In fact, the enforcers expected to be shut down entirely.

In the interim, the enforcers witnessed some horrifying things. Unable to look the other way, these civil servants became whistle-blowers. Through a friend of mine, they contacted me in August 2005. At the time, Congress was in a summer recess. But wanting to give these enforcers some political cover, I sent an invitation through the USCIS chain of command for the head of the whistle-blower group to testify before my Immigration Reform Caucus when the members returned in the fall. That, I hoped, would put the agency "on notice" that its lack of activity was under scrutiny.

My friend, meanwhile, contacted the House Judiciary Committee to set up a meeting for the whistle-blowers to appear before staffers. Unbelievably, however, those staffers went to the White House and began discussing ways to keep the agents from revealing the depth of the corruption in USCIS. The administration made it clear it did not want the information to come out for fear it would undermine the immigration guest-worker program—a plan President Bush had been pushing since 2004 that would allow undocumented workers to get three-year work visas. After all, if USCIS couldn't handle its job as it was, how could it handle a guest-worker program involving millions of people?

TURF BATTLE

WHEN THE enforcers' office was created, it was assigned just six investigators to manage a backlog of about twenty-six hundred investigations involving allegations of misconduct by USCIS agents and employees. This was on top of fourteen hundred other cases then being handled by the agency's inspector general's office, as well as an intermediate number of additional cases at ICE, the agency that was the initial intake center for all internal affairs probes when the Department of Homeland Security was first created.

It became painfully obvious that six people weren't enough for this task. Fortunately for the head of the small enforcer office, Director Aguirre had authorized the hiring of an additional twenty-three investigators. But when the enforcer office attempted to hire these investigators, USCIS threw up one obstacle after another. Anyone who had anything to do with the hiring of new personnel—human resources, the budget office, procurement—dragged their feet or stalled the process.

If the enforcers were simply trying to investigate the theft of office supplies, such intentional bureaucratic sabotage would not have been so significant. But these cases involved scandal and corruption. USCIS officials were being bribed, selling green cards, trading green cards for sex. Others were suspected of spying and espionage. There were instances of undue influence by terror-sponsoring foreign governments who publicly pretended to be America's allies. These cases involved high-level criminal activity. Many were detrimental to our national security. And those who were trying to protect our country weren't being allowed to do their jobs.

The enforcers were clear that the corruption at the agency was from top to bottom, from mail clerks to high-level management. Many of these people hailed from the old INS, where the lack of self-policing created one of the federal government's most corrupt bureaucracies ever.

One of the first things a naturalization adjudicator is supposed to do is submit the name of an applicant for a criminal background check. If any of the scores of U.S. intelligence and law-enforcement agencies has derogatory information on that applicant, the file would be flagged without specifics and returned to the adjudicator. To find out why the file was flagged, the adjudicator would call the agency with the information and then decide whether or not it was sufficient enough to deny the application.

The enforcers reported that they were aware of about fifteen hundred cases in which the criminal background check had flagged the files, noting national security information. In some of those cases, the agency that had the information—for example, the FBI, the CIA, the Defense Intelligence Agency (DIA)—refused to share it. Most of the time it was because the case was ongoing , and law enforcement does not share information with non-law-enforcement personnel. (Adjudicators are considered non-law-enforcement personnel). While that sounds crazy, the reasoning is that the USCIS office that is supposed to be the liaison with outside law-enforcement groups—the office of Fraud Detection and National Security (FDNS)—was headed by an individual who was found by the inspector general's office in 1996 to have lied to Congress in testimony. The IG recommended the administrator be charged and/or terminated. Instead, the administrator was placed in charge of the antifraud unit of USCIS.

The absurdity doesn't stop there. The same person has also posted sensitive information about ongoing cases on the Internet and reneged on promises to provide information to law-enforcement agencies. So there is no trust in him or his office.

Adjudicators, however, found a way around the system. They took the problem to the enforcers because they could obtain the information. The enforcers then informed the adjudicators if the flagged data were sufficient cause for denying the naturalization application.

When the head of FDNS learned that the adjudicators were using the enforcers to get the information, he was miffed because he was being circumvented, and this made him look bad to his superiors. So the acting deputy director of USCIS, Robert Divine—a former attorney for the American Immigration Lawyers Association, a left-wing organization that opposes sensible immigration reform—ordered the enforcers to cease sharing all information with anyone, including adjudicators. The enforcers were told not to obtain any information from outside law-enforcement agencies; they were not to share any information they had with anyone; they were forbidden from talking to the Joint Terrorism Task Force or anyone at any outside agency (e.g., FBI, CIA, DIA). All these draconian measures were implemented to ensure that the head of FDNS was still in control of his area of responsibility.

Meanwhile, the enforcers knew that some fifteen hundred cases needed to be resolved that involved people whose files had been flagged by the other agencies. And the adjudicators could not make determinations regarding those applications. In frustration, they turned to FDNS for advice and were told to approve the applicants.

In one instance, adjudicators had information from the enforcers regarding a national security case that needed to be denied. Adjudicators asked FDNS to allow them to obtain the information because the application was critical. The applicant, it was discovered, was implicated in a terrorist financing scheme. Nevertheless, FDNS instructed the adjudicator to grant the applicant citizenship status. To stop this outrage, the enforcers approached the agency's chief of staff for permission to share the crucial information with the adjudicators so that the application would be denied. They were allowed in this one instance to do so, but the enforcers were instructed never to act on such information again.

In another incident, a high-level Afghan official tried to contact DHS because his government wanted to compile a database of people in Afghan refugee camps who wanted to come to the United States but were either terrorists or had terrorist connections. But no one at DHS returned his phone calls. Why would anyone in the Department of Homeland Security want to know if a terrorist wanted to get into the country, right?

By happenstance, the Afghan official encountered one of the enforcers and told him about the database request. Of course the enforcer was interested and asked what needed to be done to get the process going. But after USCIS ordered the enforcers' office not to share any information with outside offices or foreign governments, the project was shut down.

Because of the ongoing nature of a number of enforcer investigations, some of the investigations of corruption they described were done "hypothetically." For example, suppose USCIS received a job application from a U.S. citizen who had been born in a "country of interest" in the war against terror. (Note: everyone who works for the agency domestically must be a U.S. citizen.) Suppose there was information indicating that this applicant would not be a good hire for the federal government. And suppose USCIS chose to hire this person anyway. You can imagine the kind of trouble such a person could cause in an agency responsible for issuing green cards, approving asylum requests, and doling out immigration benefits. Wouldn't such a hire create unacceptable risk factors? Remember, just nineteen terrorists carried out 9/11. One person in the right place at the right time, operating within the federal government, could ensure that an untold number of terrorist operatives could either enter or be allowed to stay in the United States.

When DHS was first created, Customs and Border Protection (CBP) was given ownership of the Treasury Enforcement Communications System (TECS) database, which is essentially a gateway to virtually all known criminal and terrorist information from various local, state and federal law-enforcement agencies. More than two-dozen agencies make their information available through TECS, including all immigration-enforcement records.

When CBP took over, an agreement stipulated that everyone who had access to TECS through the old INS system would continue to have access for two years. During this time, immigration agencies were required to upgrade and complete their background investigations so they could continue to have access to TECS after the two-year grace period passed.

This is the primary database adjudicators need to obtain terrorist watch lists, criminal records, and all national security information on applicants. But before Eduardo Aguirre arrived at the agency, someone decided that funding would not be authorized for full background investigations on all employees.

True to its word, when the two-year grace period ended on January 1, 2005, CBP terminated all access to the TECS database. USCIS dithered while adjudicators were still approving citizenship and visa applications. By the end of 2005, at least thirteen hundred adjudicators—one-third of the total number—did not have access to the TECS database.

For its part, CBP declined to approve another grace period because, among other things, the agency has had trouble in the past with unauthorized users accessing the system and using it to warn the targets of investigations and other misuses. Meanwhile, USCIS was trying to hire thousands of additional employees and still trying to figure out how to provide access to the adjudicators who must blindly decide whether a prospective employee poses a national security risk.

The territorial struggle within the agencies did not stop there. Again, as in the case at USCIS—where turf wars and incompetence are hampering efforts to secure the nation—federal agencies seem to be competing against each other over matricula consular cards.

A matricula consular card is a semiofficial form of identification issued by the Mexican government to its citizens living the United States. Though the Mexican government says otherwise, the FBI has determined it "is not a reliable form of identification."[2] Yet their use is widespread, and so far, the U.S government has done nothing to curtail their use.

Though Mexican officials claim that the cards are needed by their citizens to have so-called legitimacy while in the United States, it should be pointed out the U.S. government issues legitimate paperwork and documentation whenever it lawfully admits an alien into the country. The only reason why a Mexican citizen would need a matricula consular card from the Mexican Embassy is if they are in this country illegally.

Even more alarming, the ID cards are easy to fabricate. FBI and DHS officials have repeatedly testified that these cards are easily obtained through fraud and that they lack adequate security measures to prevent forgery. FBI officials have arrested alien smugglers with as many as seven different matricula consular cards. Authorities have even arrested an Iranian national with a Mexican matricula consular card in his own name.

The DHS and the FBI see obvious problems with matricula consular cards. But the State Department views it more "diplomatically." In early December 2005 a State Department official said that while State does not defend the use of the cards, it is concerned that limitations on the cards would provoke retaliation from other countries.[3]

In all, Mexican consulates in the United States have issued 1.2 million cards. They are accepted by hundreds of localities and local agencies around the country. Guatemala is planning on issuing similar cards to its people, and Brazil, Haiti, Nicaragua, and Poland are studying the matter.

Mexican officials explain that cards are only issued to citizens who appear in person at their embassies and consulates with acceptable identification. The FBI, however, reports that Mexican birth certificates are easy to forge, adding that many are forged because they are a key commodity in the trade of fraudulent documents. Sometimes applicants need only convince issuing officers that they are who they say they are.

Bearers of these cards, thanks to localities that are more concerned with potentially offending someone or making a dollar off of them, are allowed to blend into communities by using their cards to obtain bank accounts and some state and local services. And the federal government acts as if it's helpless to do anything. So much for national security.

In early 2006, Defense Secretary Donald Rumsfeld stated that the Pentagon's poor job of obtaining information about enemies such as al Qaeda operatives was the result of fear of media criticism.[4] "We're not going to lose wars or battles out there. The only place we can lose is if the country loses its will," he said. "And the determinant of that is what is played in the media. And, therefore, the terrorists have media committees, and they plan it. And they manipulate and manage to influence what the media carries throughout the world. And they do it very successfully. They're good at it."

The system for identifying potentially dangerous people who are trying to enter and stay in this country is clearly broken. And this is one of the main reasons for my opposition to the president's "guest-worker" program or any other program that would require DHS and USCIS to vet and clear millions of people to enter the United States. My position should be obvious to anyone after reading what these dedicated whistle-blower agents said about the inane obstacles that prevent them from doing their jobs.

All of the same problems that allowed terrorists in 2002 to be naturalized are still prevalent in today's "system" of immigration and naturalization enforcement. It's business as usual in the midst of an agency in meltdown. Corruption and incompetence severely impede our ability to determine who's coming into this country and for what purpose.

In December 2005 the DHS inspector general stated that the department was a bureaucratic mess still plagued by "major management challenges." I can't remember when I have heard a more monumental understatement.

11

Politics of Immigration

In America, we should always understand one principle. And that is: he who has the most votes dictates the public policy of this country.

—Congressman Luiz Gutierrez (D-IL)

FOR YEARS I HAVE been one of the few to voice my concern over the marriage of politics and the law. On the left side of the aisle, politicians continue to do nothing about immigration, legal or illegal, because they know their ambiguities turn into votes for them. On my side of the aisle, the Right does nothing to stop it because we believe it generates cheap labor. And the sum of those two powerful interests has stopped us from doing anything significant about the immigration problem and border security.

Our borders are porous, and they are porous because we lack the political will to close them. Neither party, however, will admit this for fear of the political retribution that would come from interest groups within the respective parties. The amazing thing is that we have the technology and the resources to secure our borders tomorrow, but we lack the political will to do it—no backbone.

Is it right and proper that our nation's borders should allow the influx of millions of people to take the jobs of American citizens? To force people either to work for less money than they were working for just a few years ago? To be unemployed? All in order to achieve the political goals described above.

There are signs that things are changing. Perhaps one of the most incredible things I have read recently indicates there has been a change in the attitude of the American people. Poll after poll now tells us that approximately 70 percent of the people are saying no to illegal immigration. A majority says that they want to see a reduction in illegal immigration until we can better control the problem.

For the longest time, the major media outlets have simply ignored the problem. But they are not alone in putting their heads in the sand. With them are the Congress and the president—be he George W. Bush or Bill Clinton. They would all prefer to ignore the fact that the American people are telling the pollsters that something has to be done about illegal immigration. Ironically, although people are upset by it, it has not been their number-one issue, and so many preferred to finesse the issue. This, of course, changed, when immigration became a priority issue.

But despite the critical security issues involved, we continue to see proposals providing amnesty for people who are living here illegally, proposals to give all kinds of benefits to people who are living here illegally, proposals that will not only teach their children in K-12 but will also provide higher education at taxpayers' expense, proposals to give illegals driver's licenses and Social Security benefits, and even proposals to let illegals vote.

GUEST-WORKER PROGRAM = AMNESTY

WHY SO many of my colleagues have bought into the lie that mass illegal immigration is a boon to the country and a benefit to their constituents is something they will have to answer for, but I also hold the Bush administration responsible for making the problem worse. I realize the difficulty of border enforcement and tight security measures has always meant America experiences more than its fair share of illegal immigration. Still, a major reason why illegals flood our country is because President Bush introduced an "immigration reform" plan in January 2004 that basically grants amnesty to millions of people who are here illegally.

The president's "guest-worker" program, which he says is *not* an amnesty but would nonetheless allow people to legally remain in the United States for a period of time to work, is at least a reward for breaking into our country. And even if it's not a full-blown amnesty, whereby any illegal alien currently in the country would be forgiven for breaking in and would be allowed to remain legally—it is being looked upon as such by the lawbreakers themselves.

Border Patrol agents reported that immediately after the president announced his plan, the number of illegal aliens coming into the United States increased dramatically—in numbers higher than previously recorded. Many who were apprehended were entering the country specifically for the "amnesty" the Bush administration was offering them.

But wait—no one in the administration has used the word *amnesty*, right? In fact, the White House vehemently denied it was offering an amnesty.

In November 2005 President Bush unveiled what he called a "comprehensive strategy to reform our immigration system." In his speech, he vowed, "Together with Congress, we're going to create a temporary-worker program that will take pressure off the border, bring workers from out of the shadows, and reject amnesty." He went on to explain: "By creating a legal channel for those who enter America to do an honest day's labor, we would reduce the number of workers trying to sneak across the border. This would free up law enforcement officials to focus on criminals, drug dealers, terrorists, and others that mean harm to us."[1]

Essentially, the president said that he was going to create a program but did not want to call it amnesty because that has a bad connotation with the public. No matter how many ways he wants to phrase it, no matter how many times he says he is against amnesty, the truth is, his plan is an amnesty plan. Here's why.

The president's plan would allow illegal aliens to stay and work in the United States for six years and then return to their country of origin. The proposed amnesty plan is "three plus three"—illegals can stay in the United States for three years as a guest worker, and then they can renew their guest worker pass for another three years.

This plan clearly offers an amnesty in two respects. First, it protects persons who have broken the law from the punishment prescribed by the law (deportation) while offering them the privilege that few get (living and working in the United States). Second, does anyone really believe that, at the end of six years, the immigrants will go home or that Congress will have the political will to make them do so? Six years from now, after we've secured the border and gotten tough on interior enforcement, there will be tremendous political pressure to go soft on the so-called guest workers who have been here for years.

For the past seven years in which I have been serving in the Congress, I have been talking about our border crisis. Every year I have proposed punitive action against localities that have illegal-alien sanctuary policies. In July 2005 I introduced the Real Guest Act (H.R. 3333) as an alternative to guest-worker programs. The proposal strove to enhance border enforcement, improve homeland security, remove incentives for illegal immigration, and establish a guest-worker program with a common-sense approach (meaning: good for America, not some other country). One reviewer commented:

> This comprehensive bill contains the toughest set of enforcement measures, border and interior. It includes meaningful employer accountability measures. The Tancredo bill creates a guest-worker program, but the enforcement measures must first go into effect and show tangible results. The guest-worker plan requires that labor market indicators must show an actual shortage of workers before foreigners can enter the U.S. workforce.[2]

While several of my colleagues in the House have expressed support for my "enforcement first" strategy, our base remains divided. Several liberal bills have been introduced that mimic the president's guest-worker program. I would rather have no bill than grant amnesty.

Amnesty is a bad policy move because no one should ever be exempt from our laws or excused from following them. That includes breaking into our country. It especially includes punishing the employers who are hiring illegals. But we allow employers to do it with millions of workers because we have learned to accept this but not that, to take this but not that, depending upon the political benefits conferred by looking the other way or pretending a problem doesn't exist. In the end, we don't consistently enforce the law—whether against the people who are breaking into this country or against Americans who are hiring the people who are here illegally. After all, the promise of a job is the primary reason so many illegal aliens come to the United States. To offer them some kind of guest-worker reward in addition to their flouting of our laws against illegal immigration is abominable.

MIXING POLITICS AND RELIGION TO GRANT AMNESTY

RECENTLY, THE issue of immigration reform morphed from a national-security issue to a politically charged issue among Washington representatives of major religious organizations. In December 2005 several religious organizations tried to institute smear tactics to prevent the passage of the House's bipartisan immigration reform bill (H.R. 4437), which calls for the construction of a security fence along our border with Mexico, requires federal and local law enforcement to cooperate on immigration matters, and mandates that employees use an instant check system to verify employees' legal status. The bill was passed in late 2005.

Claiming to speak for their churches' members, left-leaning religious activists have distorted what the bill would do and have impugned the motives of those who voted to secure the borders, claiming that bipartisan legislation does not reflect "Gospel attitudes toward immigrants." The U.S. Catholic Church, the Episcopal Church, the Evangelical Lutheran Church in America, the United Methodist Church, and the Presbyterian Church (U.S.A.) have all initiated lobbying campaigns in response to the House bill and in favor of blanket illegal-alien amnesty, despite the protests of their members who support strong border security.

Entire denominations have become embroiled in the battle for our culture, albeit—in my view—on the wrong side. For instance, few Americans know that the Catholic hierarchy in the United States is supportive of so-called immigrant rights, insofar as these religious officials back legislation protecting and encouraging mass illegal immigration as well as funding and developing "youth" programs aimed at circumventing immigration law and mocking immigration policy.

The Most Reverend Gerald R. Barnes—bishop of San Bernardino,

131

California, and chairman of the committee on migration of the U.S. Conference of Catholic Bishops (USCCB)—issued a statement on July 19, 2005, that he supported the Secure America and Orderly Immigration Act of 2005 because it represented "a comprehensive and bipartisan approach to reforming our broken immigration system." Specifically, the bishop backed the legislation's creation of "legal avenues" for migrant workers to enter the United States "in a safe and orderly manner" and its provisions for allowing "an opportunity for immigrants in the United States to work for permanent residency"—language that is code for supporting the granting of amnesty to illegal aliens already in the country.

Meanwhile, the USCCB, through its Web site, declared its opposition to another piece of legislation, the Border Protection, Antiterrorism, and Illegal Immigration Control Act of 2005, because, it said, the legislation included "many harsh provisions which would bring undue harm to immigrants and their families." Among them, the USCCB noted, were provisions that "make unlawful presence a felony; subject anyone who assists an undocumented alien to criminal penalties; require mandatory detention of all aliens apprehended along the U.S. border, including children and families; and limit relief to asylum-seekers through an expansion of expedited removal."[3] In other words, the USCCB opposes any legislation that requires the government to follow the law by criminalizing illegal entry and punishing anyone who aides in that process while also opposing the quick return of illegal immigrants to their home countries.

There is more. As part of "Suggested Activities for 'Youth,'" the *Catholic Campaign for Immigration Reform,* in its "Justice for Immigrants" parish resource pack, advises holding "a poster contest illustrating current examples of U.S. immigration laws that negatively affect immigrants or migrants." The same resource also encourages teachers to have their classes "write a bill of rights by which they would want to live. Compare these rights with the rights of (or lack thereof) immigrants. Have the class compare the United States Bill of Rights, the United Nations Declaration of Human Rights, and the Church's teaching on the rights of all people. Which is more encompassing? Stress that the Gospel alternative to the present situation is that all people would have equal access to resources to meet their basic human needs."[4]

According to the campaign's literature, "The goal of the educational activities within the parish is to promote a conversion of minds and hearts in order to bring about (1) Gospel attitudes toward immigrants, (2) a recognition that changes in public policies are needed, and (3) that parishioners have a responsibility to act upon their faith and values to promote positive change. The following suggestions for educational activities within the parish should serve to inspire creative ideas." It also advises parishes to include "immersion" activities to "community members to people whose lives differ from theirs; for example, engage in community service in a neighborhood that is culturally diverse or economically disadvantaged relative to others." And it advises priests and laypersons to include "special prayers . . . that focus on the dignity of immigrants."[5]

Teaching Americans to respect the "dignity" of immigrants is not the point of immigration reform. Americans by and large show a tremendous amount of dignity and respect to migrants—in fact, more so than most other Western nations and cultures. But these Catholic lesson plans and youth-related activities suggest that (1) all immigrants are automatically treated with disdain and disgust, and (2) that advocating tighter borders, assimilation into American culture, cracking down on employers who violate the law to hire illegal aliens, and other immigration-reform measures do an injustice to immigrants.

Radical advocates who invoke God to support an argument for blanket amnesty step over the line themselves. If we really want to be a compassionate faith community, we must enforce the law and end the border charade that lures thousands of people through the deadly desert every year. The faith community must step forward and tell leftist activists that undermining border security is not a religious imperative. I urge all churchgoers who are concerned about border security to contact the activists who insist on misrepresenting their parishioner's beliefs.

WHO'S IN CHARGE?

AFTER RECEIVING little assistance from the federal government in the battle to protect our borders, Arvin West, a small-town sheriff in Hudspeth County, Texas, decided in February 2006 that the time had come to travel to Washington DC to testify before the subcommittee on Homeland Security. "It's a two-way battle we're fighting between the drug wars, which includes Mexico's corruption," he told the *Inland Valley Daily Bulletin.* "And we're also fighting the American government to get them to listen to us. I have to find someone in the federal government who swings the big stick. In Hudspeth County, if my deputies get out of line, the buck stops with me. Where does the buck stop in Washington?"[6]

Sheriff West is not alone in the fight to help save the border counties and communities from the risks posed by illegal immigration. The Texas Sheriff's Border Coalition has also weighed in on what many describe as an apathetic government. In El Paso County, Texas, Deputy Sheriff Ryan Urrutia said, "Drug runners don't hide anymore, they confront us head on. The government has the opportunity to do something right now. If someone gets shot from across the border here or in Hudspeth County, with the way things are going, it will be too late."[7]

Consequently, several civilian volunteer groups have popped up along the border to defend their country, such as the Minutemen and the Texas Border Regulators. Both groups assist Border Patrol agents and law-enforcement officers in apprehending and deporting illegal immigrants.

Bob Masling, one of the organizers of the Texas Border Regulators, believes: "Come election time, the American people are going to base their vote on who in Washington is paying attention to this border crisis. Our community has suffered for too long, and we're just not going to take it anymore."[8]

In January 2006 the Texas Sheriff's Border Coalition announced Operation Linebacker, a project to assist Border Patrol agents in their enforcement activities along the Southwest border.[9] Fortunately, some in Washington are listening to the needs of the Americans on the border. My colleague James Sensenbrenner (R-WI) voiced his support of Operation Linebacker, vowing to ask for $100 million in funding for border-security measures.[10]

TAKE ACTION

WHILE IMMIGRATION reform continues to fuel the fires of politically charged arguments benefiting only those who maintain that illegal aliens are needed for their cheap labor and their votes, the majority of America is beginning to make their desires known. When I began speaking about immigration reform seven years ago, I argued for reform into the lonely lens of a C-SPAN camera. Today, members of Congress come up to me after they have returned from town meetings in their districts to inform me that their constituents only want to discuss the urgency for immigration reform.

It used to be that immigration reform only affected the border states. Now, no matter what state I am in, Americans want to talk about immigration reform. In Iowa recently, five hundred people waited in the pouring rain to discuss the immigration issue with me. It is to the credit of thousands of Americans who have raised their voices on this issue that we are beginning to play offense for the first time. Every time I turn on a radio, every time I turn on a television, every time I pick up a newspaper, someone is debating immigration.

While immigration has gone from taboo to a common thing to talk about, we are far from reaching the goal. There is an incredible amount of work to be done. With your help, this issue will be settled. It will be dealt with through a democratic process and in a way that will make us proud of that process. It is a tough, controversial, emotional issue. But we must talk about it. Contact your representatives and senators. You must voice your desire for a secure nation for you and your family. And more important, I urge my colleagues in Congress to pass legislation that defends our borders. We cannot continue to ignore the majority of Americans who want national security just so we can satisfy pressure groups with their own political motives. Our nation has too much at stake to become the fateful pawn in a political game of chess.

12

Breach in Security

What more will it take before "never again" is more than just an empty rhetorical mantra to pacify the American public?

—Michelle Malkin, syndicated columnist

UNDER CURRENT DEPARTMENT OF Homeland Security guidelines, there is no doubt that terrorists have been given free access to our country though we are supposedly spending a fortune to "do everything in our power" to keep them out. In fact, we are *not* keeping these people out. We are continuously showing the terrorists that we are content to allow them to enter our country and do God only knows what to our homeland. One such example took place just six months after 9/11: immigration officials sent notices to two of the 9/11 hijackers that they had been approved for flight school visas. This oversight outraged a mourning nation, and President Bush and Washington officials vowed that this type of blunder would never happen again. But 9/11 and this blunder were not enough to prevent this same situation from happening again.

On January 15, 2005, immigration officials sent a notice to Eugueni Kniazev, an immigrant from Siberia, that he had become a "lawful permanent resident of the United States."[1] Unfortunately, Kniazev was one of the victims killed in the attacks on the World Trade Center in 2001. A little more than three years after his death, a deceased foreigner received U.S. citizenship. If our own agencies cannot keep track of who is in our country, how can we expect those charged with our protection to guarantee "never again" when it comes to terrorism?

While the snafus within the homeland security and immigration agencies are allowing terrorists into the country, there are thousands of unaccounted illegals with unfettered access to things that could aid in the terrorists' goal of death and destruction to America.

NUCLEAR FACILITY COMPROMISED

THE Y-12 National Security Complex near Oak Ridge, Tennessee, plays a significant role in the Department of Energy's nuclear-weapons programs. The Y-12 complex is charged with "strengthening national security and reducing the global threat from weapons of mass destruction."[2] Constructed during World War II as part of the Manhattan Project, the Y-12 complex was responsible for separating uranium 235 to be used in "Little Boy," the atomic bomb dropped on Hiroshima. Since then, Y-12 has become a "high-precision manufacturing, assembly, and inspection facility while maintaining the nation's uranium and lithium technology base."[3]

In its national defense role, the facility is responsible for the production of nuclear-weapons components; receipt, storage, and protection of nuclear materials; surveillance of the U.S. nuclear-weapons stockpiles; and dismantling weapons and weapons components. One would think that this facility, which is commonly placed on high alert due to its sensitive nature, would take every measure possible to ensure that illegal immigrants would not gain access to the complex. One would be wrong.

In June 2005 the Energy Department's inspector general revealed "non-U.S. citizens were improperly allowed access to a leased facility at the Department of Energy's Y-12 complex in Oak Ridge, Tennessee." In his report, Inspector General Gregory H. Friedman detailed the shocking results of the inspection:

> We found that foreign construction workers, using false documents, had, in fact, gained access to the Y-12 site on multiple occasions. Specifically, 16 foreign construction workers were found to

have been illegal aliens. Some of these workers acquired facility access badges and were, as a result, permitted access to the main Y-12 site. Others were able to access an adjacent Y-12 leased facility.

Certain information associated with the construction of the Y-12 leased facility, which was planned to store documents up to the Secret–Restricted Data level was considered Unclassified Controlled Nuclear Information (UCNI) and Official Use Only (OUO). Consequently, these individuals may have had opportunities to inappropriately access this type of information.

As if this were not bad enough, the report also revealed: "The Office of Counterintelligence was not aware of the presence of foreign construction workers at the Y-12 leased facility until notified by the Office of Inspector General during this inspection. Counterintelligence had not been performed for these individuals to that point."[4]

What does it say about our intelligence community and law enforcement when illegal aliens not only get past the Y-12 gates but also then gain access to top-secret materials? None of this should come as a surprise after a 2004 simulated terrorist attack revealed significant lapses in security at the Y-12 complex.

Inspectors at the Y-12 plant were shocked to learn that security guards were able to repel "four simulated terrorist attacks—a feat computer programs predicted wouldn't be done."[5] It was later learned that an outside security contractor tipped the guards to the forthcoming drills, allowing them to cheat in the mock attacks. Consequently, Inspector General Friedman and his investigators learned, "This was a pattern of actions . . . going back to the mid-1980s that may have negatively affected the reliability of site performance testing." Not only was eighty-five thousand dollars wasted in the staged attack, but also it became painfully obvious that security was not a top priority for one of the Department of Energy's "most sensitive sites."

PORT SECURITY BROUGHT TO YOU BY THE UNITED ARAB EMIRATES

WHILE IT is next to impossible to keep track of every foreign illegal in the United States, one thing we should be able to secure and monitor is our ports. One of the most vulnerable targets for terrorists, it has been revealed that more must be been done to secure our seaports.

Government inspectors revealed in mid-2005 that only 17.5 percent of high-risk shipping containers were being inspected.[6] Also disclosed was the failure of a DHS program that allowed approved traders expedited import-export time; the government had vetted only 11 percent of the traders.[7]

With ninety-five thousand miles of open shoreline and 361 ports, the majority of the cargo that moves in and out of the country is received and shipped through our ports. A House subcommittee reported, "Each year more than 7,500 commercial vessels make approximately 51,000 port calls, and over six million loaded marine containers enter U.S. ports."[8] Cargo containers can be easily transferred from ships to semitrucks or railcars and moved to virtually any area of the nation. The volume and accessibility of cargo containers provides the ideal method for terrorists to transport any number of weapons around the country. So why would we hand over control of some of our ports to an Arab nation?

The federal government announced in February 2006 the Dubai government's $6.8 billion acquisition of Peninsular and Oriental Steam Navigation Company of London, making the company "the world's third-largest port operator, with 51 terminals in 30 countries," including six ports in the United States.[9] Dubai, a country in the United Arab Emirates, has known ties to terrorists and the 9/11 hijackers, which raised concerns about national security—and rightly so.

The port company operates shipping terminals at ports in Baltimore, Miami, New York, New Jersey, New Orleans, and Philadelphia.[10] The deal, which was approved by the Committee on Foreign Investment in the United States, would have given a foreign country access to the United States. This, after many of the 9/11 hijackers entered our nation via the United Arab Emirates. Investigators of the 9/11 tragedy concluded that "much of the attack's planning was done there, and the FBI says money for the operation was transferred to the hijackers primarily through the UAE's banking system."[11] It was also well known that the United Arab Emirates had provided support for the insurgency in Iraq. So why would we allow our enemies the access they so desperately desire in their drive to destroy the West? This op-ed from the *Washington Times* said it all:

> We should be improving port security in an age of terrorism, not outsourcing decisions to the highest bidder. The ports are thought to be the country's weakest homeland-security link, with good reason. Only a fraction of the nation's maritime cargoes are inspected.
>
> This deal appears to be all about money.

Unbelievably, the Bush administration defended the transaction under sharp criticism by those concerned with our national security. In an interview amid the controversial decision, Homeland Security Secretary Michael Chertoff said, "We have to balance the paramount urgency of security against the fact that we still want to have a robust global trading system." Fortunately, Dubai pulled out of the deal after it became controversial.

THEATER OF THE ABSURD

THE AFOREMENTIONED incidents are just a few of the many bizarre and unbelievable breaches in national security that have occurred since 9/11. Listed below is a small sample of other national security threats that have fallen through the cracks:

- December 2002: An illegal alien using fraudulent documents was able to deceive federal agents while working at the White House. Evading the White House and Secret Service, a routine fingerprint and immigration database check led to the arrest of Salvador Martinez-Gonzalez and a return trip to Mexico.[12]
- November 2003: New York City police issued an alert after explosives powerful enough to take down a commercial jetliner were reported missing.[13]
- July 2004: The national security chief at Los Alamos National Laboratory in New Mexico announced an investigation into the disappearance of two computer drives with "classified data on nuclear weapons." Los Alamos is where the atomic bomb was developed.[14]

- July 2004: Department of Homeland Security Undersecretary Asa Hutchinson publicly stated it was "not realistic" for officers to conduct enforcement sweeps and deport illegal lawbreakers.[15]
- August 2004: Robert Bonner, commissioner of U.S. Border and Customs Protection Rights, issued a memo detailing training sessions for border agents to be more polite. The training sessions included instructions on etiquette, grooming, body language, housekeeping, maintaining food perishables in the workplace, and communications skills.[16]
- January 2005: By court order, the District of Columbia handed over security data to the International Action Center, a protest group with ties to known terrorist groups. WorldNetDaily.com reported that more than "1,000 pages of documents, 38 videotapes and numerous photographs and audiotapes related to D.C. police tactics, training, planning and the 2001 presidential inauguration are now in the hands of IAC, which has ties to FARC and the National Liberation Army, both of which the State Department describes as terrorist organizations."[17]
- April 2005: Breaching British security, Abdoul Masmoud Yessoufou was arrested after he was able to sneak on board the USS *Harry S. Truman* while it made a port call in Portsmouth, England.[18]

These are just a handful of the *known* national security breaches. We continue to allow breaches like these and many others by simply not enforcing the law. Instead, we make a mockery of it by making sure Border Patrol agents are courteous to those who wish to kill us.

13

Mexico's Lawless Border

So our proposal is to move to a second phase of NAFTA where in five to ten years that border will be open to the free flow of people, workers, transiting the border between our two countries, same as we're doing with products, services, and merchandise.

—Mexican President Vicente Fox[1]

IN HIS BOOK, *The Next War,* the late Reagan administration defense secretary Caspar Weinberger predicted that by 2003 the United States would be at war with Mexico. Continued social unrest along the border regions, exacerbated by drug trafficking and illegal immigration, would eventually lead Washington and Mexico City to blows, he wrote. While that scenario has yet to play out, there are signs that "Cap" knew what he was talking about. While we are not fighting a conventional war, we are still in a battle to protect our borders by fighting a war of sovereignty.

Although Mexican President Vicente Fox and others often speak of attempting to do something to reduce the flow of immigrants to the United States, in reality they only encourage it. Fox "dreams of a day when the border will open and his countrymen will no longer flee to survive."

The Mexican president need dream no longer. There is little preventing the free flow of illegals into this country from Mexico. Not only is Fox not attempting to stop it, but he and his government are abetting it.

Due to bureaucratic red tape and corruption inherent in Mexican law-enforcement agencies, the one-hundred-person Houston Task Force on Terrorism reported that it had to sift through thousands of terrorist-related tips and pieces of evidence without the kind of logistical support they expected from an ally and neighbor. One task-force source noted that the Mexican security community, especially the Center for Investigations and National Security, was still mired in political corruption and that members in President Fox's own administration insist they should be informed about any high-priority intelligence before it is passed on to U.S. authorities. The Fox administration has been suppressing information that might reveal the actual size of anti-U.S. terror cells in Mexico City and their connection to militant Muslim groups around Mexico and in many Latin American hot spots.

"Our Mexican and American officials are working together to arrest dangerous criminals, including drug smugglers and those who traffic in human beings. President Fox and I are determined to protect the safety of American people and the Mexican people,"[2] President Bush announced in March 2004 as he and Fox mingled at the president's Crawford, Texas, ranch. In contrast, U.S. officials have yet to see that kind of cooperation. Instead, the Mexican government distributes kits to illegals preparing to cross the border. Designed to make their trip easier, they include water, condoms, Band-Aids, maps, and food supplies for a day or so. At the same time, President Fox tells us that they are trying to help reduce the flow of immigrants into the United States.

In early 2006 Mexico's Human Rights Commission planned to distribute about seventy thousand maps to illegal border-crossers along with a guide to the expected risks. The poster-size maps "use red dots to pinpoint where hundreds of immigrants have died. Blue flags indicate where the 70 water tanks placed by Humane Borders are, and stars show where U.S. Border Patrol rescue beacons are located."[3] Incidentally, the Human Rights Commission, a Mexican-government-funded agency, suspended distribution of the maps after it was believed that anti-immigrant groups like the Minutemen might utilize the map to help capture illegals. "This would be practically like telling the Minutemen where the migrants are going to be," said Miguel Ángel Paredes, spokesman for the Human Rights Commission. "We are going to rethink this, so that we wouldn't almost be handing them over to groups that attack immigrants."[4]

This incident was not the first time the Mexican government sought to provide information for would-be illegals about entry into the United States. In January 2005 Mexico's Foreign Ministry published a thirty-two-page comic book titled *The Guide for the Mexican Migrant*. The handbook provided tips with illustrations for situations such as:

- To cross the river can be very risky, above all if you cross alone and at night.
- If you cross by desert, try to walk at times when the heat will not be too intense.
- If you get lost, guide yourself by lightposts, train tracks, or dirt roads.
- If you decide to hire people traffickers to cross the border, consider the following precautions: Do not let them out of your sight. Remember that they are the only ones who know the lay of the land, and therefore the only ones who can get you out of that place.
- It is better to be arrested for a few hours and repatriated to Mexico than to get lost in the desert.[5]

Of course, some U.S. lawmakers were absolutely stunned by the Mexican government's willingness to aid illegal immigration. Arizona Representative J. D. Hayworth's reaction was "more astonishment than anger that a government that claims to want to be an active partner in preventing illegal immigration is an active and willing accomplice to engendering more illegal immigration."[6]

This was certainly not the act of a friendly neighbor. How would the Mexican government respond if we encouraged our citizens to violate Mexican law? It is a great example of how hooked Mexico has become on remittances—dollars sent home by alien nationals in the United States. Remittances are now about eighteen billion dollars per year and account for more income to Mexico than any source other than oil exports.

Ironically, when the United States was considering actions to secure the border by building a security fence in 2005, Fox called the policy "shameful," adding, "Mexico is not going to bear, it is not going to permit, and it will not allow a stupid thing like this wall."

Although I am disturbed by Mexico's intentional, premeditated circumvention of U.S. immigration laws, I am no longer surprised. Fox's former foreign secretary told a Senate committee that Mexico would not cooperate with the United States unless we allowed an ever-increasing flow of laborers into our country. In addition to producing step-by-step guides for entering the United States illegally, the Mexican military routinely crosses onto U.S. soil, which violates every domestic and international law on the books.

INCURSIONS ON THE INCREASE

MEXICO HAS long been a haven for violent drug cartels as well as the primary source for most illegal immigration into the United States. But in recent years, suspected Mexican paramilitary and military units, loyal to the drug cartels, have made repeated armed incursions into the United States—all with the knowledge of our government. The Department of Homeland Security has documented 231 incursions from 1996 to 2005 involving Mexican military, state, or municipal police units. And more than a few U.S. officials believe that some of the Latin American drug cartels may be operating in support of our terrorist enemies.

In 2001 alone, twenty-three incursions were documented by the Border Patrol and other law-enforcement agencies, nine of them involving Mexican military troops. State and local police units accounted for the other fourteen incursions (see map on page 147).

These raids feature squads dressed in Mexican army clothing, traveling in military-type Humvees. As noted above, the Department of Homeland Security has admitted there have been more than two hundred documented incursions by Mexican military or police—or drug or people smugglers dressed in military uniforms; there are no estimates of how many undocumented incidents have occurred. According to DHS, several Border Patrol agents have been wounded in these encounters.

In early 2006 the number of incursions rose dramatically after the Border Patrol slightly increased the number of agents and updated its

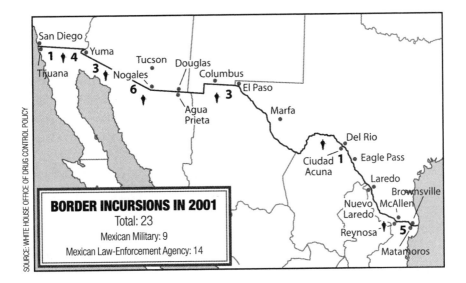

San Diego
Yuma
1 4
Tijuana
3 Nogales
Tucson
Douglas
Columbus
6
El Paso
3
Agua
Prieta
Marfa
Del Rio
Ciudad **1** Eagle Pass
Acuna
Laredo
Brownsville
Nuevo McAllen
Laredo
Reynosa **5**
Matamoros

BORDER INCURSIONS IN 2001
Total: 23
Mexican Military: 9
Mexican Law-Enforcement Agency: 14

technology at key points along the border. In need of more and better firepower to smuggle their "products" into the United States, the cartels and other criminal enterprises utilized more Mexican military-type units.

These incursions have become such routine occurrences that the Bureau of Customs and Border Protection now issues a wallet card known as the SALUTE card to Border Patrol agents. The card is a list of what agents should do when they encounter uniformed Mexican personnel on U.S. territory. SALUTE is an acronym for what agents are to observe and report about such incidents: size (of the unit), activity, location, unit, time, and equipment. The card also reminds U.S. personnel, "Remember: Mexican Army personnel are trained to evade, escape, and counter-ambush if necessary to escape."

Two recent events in Texas and California highlight the challenge the United States faces on its southern border. They not only illustrate how vulnerable the border is to drug smuggling but also how difficult it is to get the Mexican government to cooperate with our efforts to control the smuggling.

On January 23, 2006, three SUVs were seen fording the Rio Grande at Neely's Crossing. Hudspeth County, Texas, sheriff's deputies gave chase, and the SUVs turned back and headed toward the river. There the caravan was met by a military-style Humvee with a mounted .50-caliber machine gun on the U.S. side of the river. One SUV blew a tire short of the river and was abandoned by the smugglers. One made it back across the river, but the third got stuck. A dozen men in battle-dress uniforms with AK-47 rifles appeared on the Mexican side of the river and helped to unload many bales of contraband from the marooned SUV. The sheriff's deputies and highway patrol officers could only watch because they were outgunned and outmanned. After unloading their cargo, the Mexicans set fire to the SUV, leaving it to burn in the riverbed.

Two days later, in Tijuana, Mexico, a sophisticated eight-hundred-yard tunnel was found under the U.S.-Mexico border. Discovered near the Tijuana airport, the tunnel ran to a warehouse in the United States. The warehouse sheltered two trucks and a van, and the tunnel contained four tons of marijuana. Authorities said that four tunnels had been uncovered in the area in recent months. The latest discovered tunnel contained a cement floor and was large enough for people to walk through upright.

Hudspeth County, Texas, Sheriff Arvin West was convinced that the Humvee with the mounted machine gun at Neely's Crossing as well as the dozen men in military-style uniforms were elements of the Mexican military. West has lived on the border all his life, speaks Spanish fluently, and has had considerable interaction with the Mexican military and Mexican police over the years.

West and several Border Patrol agents have seen dozens of similar Mexican military incursions into the United States occur in connection with drug smuggling. Many of the sixteen county sheriffs who make up the Texas Border Sheriff's Coalition have a catalog of stories about similar incidents involving Mexican military forces along the Rio Grande.

The Mexican government's reaction to the reports of the incident was predictable: a mixture of denial and confusion. At first, Mexican authorities said that their military had no Humvees in its arsenal and that the smugglers were using stolen military equipment and uniforms. Mexican foreign minister Luis Derbez then said that the smugglers might have been U.S. troops disguised as Mexicans. And then the Mexican government reported that its military forces had been ordered not to approach within three kilometers of the border.

Most disturbing, however, was the official U.S. response. DHS Secretary Michael Chertoff downplayed the events by saying that most Mexican military incursions over the years had been "accidental." The FBI was quoted by Mexican media as saying it supported the view that the uniformed personnel were smugglers and not Mexican military.

Consider the ramifications of these two reactions. First, does the Mexican government want us to believe that the drug cartels can operate freely along the border with stolen military vehicles, weapons, and uniforms, and the Mexican military is powerless to stop them? Do DHS and the State Department want us to believe that Hudspeth County law-enforcement eyewitnesses are ignorant or incapable of identifying Mexican military vehicles and uniforms? Is the U.S. government intent on ignoring the extent of the corruption and the involvement of the Mexican military in the multibillion-dollar drug-smuggling business? Of course not. Sadly, the federal government is more concerned about allowing the Mexican government to save face than it is about telling the truth to the American people.

Since Mexico now admits it is unable to control its border, it's time the Border Patrol and local law enforcement be given the weapons to match the firepower of the cartels. New rules of engagement are necessary to allow them to return fire and also engage the smugglers intercepted on this side of the border. Law enforcement should not have to stand by as mere observers while smugglers recover their cargo on the southern bank of the Rio Grande.

It is widely understood by law-enforcement agencies, the Border Patrol, the FBI, and the DEA that high-ranking members of the Mexican military in the border regions are often bribed to cooperate in the drug cartels' operations. The corruption of Mexican law-enforcement agencies is pervasive and systemic. And honest police officers and military commanders find themselves under constant threat; they are frequently the victims of violence and even assassination.

It is hard to believe that eight-hundred-yard tunnels can be excavated, equipped, and operated without the knowledge and cooperation of Tijuana law enforcement. How many hundreds of thousands of illegal aliens of various nationalities are being smuggled into California through such tunnels? Those tunnels are not only a problem for drug enforcement, they are a serious threat to our national security.

In February 2006 federal agents and local police officers seized several caches of weapons near Laredo, Texas. Intercepted were two completed bombs and materials for thirty-three more, three hundred primers, almost four thousand rounds of ammunition, five grenade shells, nine pipe bombs with end caps, twenty-six grenade triggers, thirty-one grenade spoons, forty grenade pins, nineteen black-powder casings, ninety-one firearm magazines, four silencers, six kits of unassembled automatic weapons, twenty assembled firearms (including AK-47s and AR-15s), two Uzi assault weapons, two bulletproof vests, sniper scopes, police scanners, pinhole cameras, and other pistols and rifles. Also found were cocaine, methamphetamines, four hundred pounds of marijuana, and five thousand dollars in cash. Immigration and Customs Enforcement (ICE) agents describes the bombs as improvised explosive devices, the formal designation for homemade devices often used in unconventional warfare by terrorists, guerrillas, or commando forces.[7] Drug cartels have been known to use weapons and tactics similar to those of the terrorists, but in terms of bolstering border security, what does it matter who left the weapons? Armed drug-runners and terrorists represent an equal danger to American citizens.

While the Mexican government has, of course, emphatically denied its army is involved in any cross-border incursions, members of U.S. law enforcement as well as some federal law-enforcement personnel know better. They are convinced that the Mexican units seen on American soil are employing their specialized skills in support of drug, weapons, and human smuggling.

Even more disturbing is that this lack of cooperation doesn't come cheap. Since 2000, U.S. spending on military and police aid to Mexico has risen from $16.3 million to $57.8 million.[8] Unfortunately, this increase has not translated into results. The Mexican government has never believed that securing its border with the United States was a priority. Consequently, much of the equipment and resources we have given to Mexico to combat terrorism hasn't produced positive results. Since 9/11, the United States has sent ten x-ray machines, sixteen of fifty-seven various helicopters promised to Mexico, $13 million in computer equipment, ten motorcycles, and twelve pickups.[9] Ironically, of the helicopters given to Mexico since 2001, none has been stationed near the border as of December 2005.[10] Instead, Mexico has become a coconspirator in other areas pertaining to border security, such as immigrant smuggling.

THE MADRINAS

THERE IS an institution in Mexico that exists in some form in many third-world countries: the "Madrinas" system. It is likely that the Mexican military personnel that were spotted at Neely's Crossing were shadowy proxy criminals known as Madrinas. They are described as operating in the shadows because there is no formal organization, no union, no headquarters, no membership list, no leader. They can be described as proxies because they never undertake an activity without orders or permission from some government official. They are not freelance operators.

Officially recognized Mexican government employees are known as funcionarios. They are commissioned and recognized by a Mexican government agency, civilian or military. To augment these employees, officers of specific jurisdictions appoint others to function under the cover of their authority. These appointees are the Madrinas. (The word refers to a godmother or guardian angel.) Thus, Madrinas are an arm of the government but not officially part of the government. They are corrupt police chiefs and unofficial agents representing government officials.

Madrinas are not listed on any personnel roster, draw no salary, and get no benefits, but they act as if they are government employees. They often wear uniforms, carry government identification, and obtain equipment from legitimate agencies. Their credentials would be considered "honorary" in the United States, but a honorary cop here has no authority and is appointed to an honorary position for political purposes only. The Madrinas, however, carry the full force of legitimacy. They also have one very special quality: they are expendable. Government officials who use Madrinas to do their dirty work have "plausible deniability."

Madrinas are paid through the "mordida," or bribes, they collect. In turn, Madrinas give a large percentage of the mordida to their sponsoring government officials. Thus the incentive and necessity for criminal activity is built into the system, and drug smuggling has become a large part of the Madrinas' livelihood in the border regions.

There are several advantages to employing Madrinas:

1. There is no payroll.
2. There are no official benefits.
3. There are no records. Officially, Madrinas don't exist.
4. If there are complications of any sort, Madrinas are expendable.
5. When Madrinas are used, one can always disavow any relation to any activity. There are no records, no official authority, no accountability, no culpability.
6. Madrinas can be used as an intermediary between officials and the drug cartels.
7. When Madrinas are used, there are no photographs, letters, phone calls, or witnesses who can connect any government official with the criminal elements.
8. In serious cases of corruption or malfeasance, when someone must identified and punished, Madrinas can be scapegoats. They can be murdered, and an official can be portrayed as the hero for ending the problem.
9. If Madrinas are apprehended in the possession of government equipment (military vehicles, weapons, supplies, clothing, documents), they can be labeled as thieves and counterfeiters.
10. Madrinas do the dirty work so the authorities can remain above reproach.
11. Madrinas are usually chosen from the most brutal, morally depraved, meanest individuals in the community. Many have criminal records and have been imprisoned in the United States, Mexico, or both.
12. Since Madrinas are recruited from local thugs, the legitimate agency can co-opt the local criminal element into channeling their efforts into mutually beneficial activities. This allows an agency to avoid the embarrassment of escalating local crime statistics on file in Mexico City.
13. Madrinas have no retirement plan. They usually have a short life span. But the pay is exceptional.

Madrinas are good informants because they have loyalty to no one but themselves. U.S. law enforcement and Border Patrol agents have been able to gain information from several of them. And many Madrinas are killed by their Mexican sponsors for having informed on their activities or for holding back too much mordida or skimming drug loads.

Madrinas may or may not have criminal records when they are first recruited, but their subsequent activities are never considered as crimes, and they do not run the risk of having a criminal record as long as they function well as a Madrina. If a Madrina decides to emigrate to the United States, he can usually enter legally by obtaining a visa or border crossing card. Any criminal record he might have had can often be destroyed through a small bribe to one of his government friends. Additionally, if a Madrina tried to enter the United States illegally and were caught, he could have no criminal record on file that can be identified by U.S. authorities. And Mexico has no central registry of criminals or warrants like the FBI's National Crime Information Center (NCIC).

It is somewhat surprising that neither the Border Patrol nor any U.S. official has brought up the possibility that Madrinas were responsible for the highly publicized incident at Neely's Crossing. Certainly the intelligence unit of the Border Patrol and the FBI are aware of the Madrinas system and their involvement in the drug-smuggling business. Perhaps the Bush administration does not want to embarrass Mexican president Vicente Fox by discussing this topic publicly.

Whatever the reason for the U.S. government's silence on this question, avoiding a discussion of the Madrinas problem merely plays into the Mexican government's strategy of denial. The Madrinas system is a huge embarrassment and a grave problem that will not be overcome anytime soon, but openly discussing it is a first step toward dealing with it.

The important point is that Madrinas cannot function without the official sanction of whatever agency they are working for. They are not independent, freelance criminals. Thus, the Mexican government was involved in the Texas incident through its military, but it has plausible deniability through the convenience of Madrinas. In this case, like so many others, Madrinas served the purpose for which they are designed.

But not all border incursions identified as the Mexican army are the work of Madrinas. In the view of local law enforcement and many

Border Patrol agents, the Mexican army is solely responsible for numerous violations of U.S. sovereignty. But whether a particular incident was perpetrated by military units or by Madrinas serving as the army's proxy, the Mexican government bears responsibility.

Why the U.S. government insists on minimizing the Mexican government's involvement in these incursions is a good question. The true character and extent of the lawlessness on the Mexican side of the border needs to be understood by the American public as part of the debate over border security. Any "security partnership" with Mexico must take into account the fact that the Mexican government chooses to overlook the incipient anarchy within its borders and is unable to control elements of its government that are on the payroll of the drug cartels.

The Mexican government must stop making excuses, and the U.S. government must start being honest with the American public. It is time for our government leaders to confront the problem honestly and effectively—our future depends on it.

14

The Economics of Mass Migration

We hear claims that immigrants are somehow bad for the economy—even though this economy could not function without them.

—President George W. Bush, State of the Union, 2006

CONTRARY TO THE PROTESTATIONS of the open-borders crowd, illegal immigration does not result in a net economic benefit to the United States. In fact, illegal immigration and, for that matter, legal mass migration cost American taxpayers far more than it generates annually.

It is continuously argued that illegal immigrants benefit our economy because they provide a bountiful low-wage labor pool that helps to keep down the costs of domestically produced goods and services. And because they contribute mightily to federal, state, and local tax coffers, they consume far less in public funds than they contribute.

Nothing could be farther from the truth.

Without belaboring the point that an abundance of low-skilled, low-wage-earning, poorly educated migrants is destroying the American labor market (and thereby weakening tax collections), let's instead concentrate on the lie that mass migration produces a wealth of economic benefits for the country. In terms of tax payments, the purchasing of goods and services, and other forms of revenue versus public-funds usage, immigration costs U.S. taxpayers in excess of

155

seventy billion dollars annually.[1] Most of these costs are borne by state and local governments, while the majority of tax receipts paid for immigrants by employers go to the federal government. Aside from making use of public-welfare benefits, illegal aliens also generate huge government expenditures for education, criminal justice, and emergency and nonemergency medical care.

According to a study by the Federation for American Immigration Reform (FAIR), which supports a reduction of legal migration, "The cost of immigration to our society is enormous." Based on Census Bureau figures, FAIR noted, "We are admitting over one million mostly poor people into our society every year—a society that is already challenged to deal with the poverty of its natives."

THE COST OF EDUCATION

K–12 EDUCATION to children of illegal immigrants costs states more than twelve billion dollars annually.[2] These costs are heaped on local districts at a time when they are straining to make ends meet, at a time when schools are facing drastic cuts in funding on the state level. At the same time these districts are also bearing increases in the cost of education materials, feeding students, and paying for infrastructure—utilities, sports programs, busing. Throw into the mix other special programs, such as those for non-English-speaking students, supplemental food programs for poor immigrant families, and other ancillary expenditures, and you can begin to appreciate why educating some 1.5 million school-aged illegal aliens and their 2 million U.S.-born siblings costs so much (see the chart on page 157).[3]

In the end, *all* children—those of illegal aliens and American children alike—are receiving poorer educations because of the extra immigration-related costs. Our children will suffer in the long run when they are unable to prepare for college and/or secure better-paying, high-skilled jobs.

THE COST OF INCARCERATION

ADVOCATES FOR immigration reform have said that a large part of the problem with mass migration is that the United States often winds up

SOURCE: DIGEST OF EDUCATION STATISTICS 2002, NATIONAL CENTER FOR EDUCATION STATISTICS, U.S. DEPARTMENT OF EDUCATION

ESTIMATED COSTS OF EDUCATING ILLEGAL ALIEN STUDENTS AND U.S.-BORN CHILDREN OF ILLEGAL ALIENS IN 2004
(in $ millions)

State	Illegal Alien Students	U.S-Born Children of Illegal Aliens	Total	State	Illegal Alien Students	U.S-Born Children of Illegal Aliens	Total
California	3,220.2	4,508.3	7,728.5	Kansas	80.2	112.3	192.5
Texas	1,645.4	2,303.6	3,949.0	Utah	76.8	107.6	184.4
New York	1,306.3	1,828.9	3,135.2	Ohio	76.3	106.9	183.2
Illinois	834.0	1,167.6	2,001.7	Oklahoma	67.1	94.0	161.1
New Jersey	620.2	868.2	1,488.4	Tennessee	65.0	91.0	156.0
Florida	518.1	725.3	1,243.4	New Mexico	63.8	89.3	153.2
Georgia	396.7	555.3	952.0	South Carolina	59.88	83.7	143.5
North Carolina	321.3	449.8	771.1	Nebraska	43.4	60.7	104.1
Arizona	311.8	436.5	748.3	Iowa	41.3	57.8	99.1
Colorado	235.0	329.1	564.1	Arkansas	37.3	52.2	89.5
Washington	228.9	320.5	549.4	Missouri	36.8	51.5	88.3
Massachusetts	206.0	288.5	494.5	Rhode Island	36.4	51.0	87.4
Virginia	188.7	264.2	452.9	Alabama	34.4	48.1	82.5
Oregon	167.4	234.4	401.8	Idaho	27.3	38.2	65.5
Michigan	135.4	189.5	324.9	Delaware	22.4	31.4	53.8
Nevada	133.8	187.3	321.1	Kentucky	21.5	30.1	51.7
Maryland	117.0	163.8	280.8	Washington DC	19.6	27.5	47.1
Minnesota	115.2	161.3	276.6	Other States*	12.4	17.4	29.8
Pennsylvania	99.9	139.9	239.9	Alaska	11.3	15.8	27.0
Connecticut	95.2	133.3	228.5	Mississippi	9.9	13.8	23.7
Indiana	85.9	120.3	206.2	Louisiana	7.3	10.2	17.5
Wisconsin	83.9	117.5	201.4	Hawaii	3.0	4.2	7.2

*Maine, Montana, New Hampshire, North Dakota, South Dakota, Vermont, West Virginia, and Wyoming

importing much of the world's poverty. The same argument can be made regarding the world's criminals. Not every illegal immigrant who comes to the United States is a poor, downtrodden soul merely looking for a better life. Many are criminals who continue their crime-ridden lifestyles in America.

Some of the most violent criminals running free in the United States today are illegal immigrants. Even more disturbing, in cities and communities where illegal immigrants concentrate, police are prevented from using the best tool available to apprehend them: their illegal immigrant status.[4] According to a mid-2004 study, 95 percent of all outstanding warrants for homicides in Los Angeles targeted illegal aliens; up to two-thirds of all fugitive felony warrants (seventeen thousand) are for illegals.[5]

Most of the cost of incarcerating illegal alien criminals falls to state and local governments; the federal government only reimburses, on average, about 25 percent of these costs through the Department of Justice's State Criminal Alien Assistance Program (SCAAP). Worse, the federal government has been reducing the funding for this program. Funds for SCAAP were cut from $550 million in 2002 to $250 million in 2003. In fiscal year 2005, funding had risen slightly to $300 million. In all, the United States spent nearly $5.8 billion incarcerating illegal aliens between 2002 and 2005.[6]

In addition to this figure, the United States spent more than $12 billion on direct border-enforcement operations in fiscal year 2006 alone—nearly one-third of the Department of Homeland Security's $40 billion budget.[7]

THE COST OF CHEAP LABOR

AMERICANS HAVE voiced concern that cracking down on illegal immigration would impact certain industries, such as agriculture, because it would rob those industries of workers who are both willing and able to do the jobs they require—jobs, they say, Americans don't want. I am not averse to these concerns, but as I indicated earlier in this book, I'm not convinced they are completely valid, either.

There are Americans all over the country who are either unemployed or underemployed. Many people in my district, for example, were initially trained for high-tech jobs, but now they drive cabs at night to earn a living. That's because big corporations have been outsourcing their jobs—in the name of free trade—to other nations whose workers cost less. Outsourcing has forced many Americans to take jobs of *any* kind in order to keep a roof over their heads and food on the table. But Americans are unable to find even those jobs because they are going to illegal aliens—and for far less than what you and I would consider "prevailing" wages.

So let's be clear about what is really going on in terms of jobs "Americans won't do": (1) they aren't shunning those jobs, they are shunning the bottom-of-the-barrel wages those jobs pay; and (2) those jobs are paying bottom-of-the-barrel wages because they are going to low-skilled illegal workers who are willing to do them for far less than an American worker needs to live.

The right question is not why someone will not take a six-dollar-an-hour job when he or she needs ten dollars or twenty dollars an hour to live. The right question is how can they take such a cut in pay and survive? Six bucks an hour might be good money to an illegal alien who has little prospect of making similar wages back home and is sharing a one-room shack with ten people, but it is not good pay by American living standards. After Americans have, for generations, fought for and won a better standard of living, why should they be expected to give it up so noncitizens can work? It's absurd.

American workers' wages will never rise as long as there are illegal aliens willing to do certain jobs for below-average wages. Economists have repeatedly asserted that increased illegal immigration continues to have a massive wage-depreciating effect on U.S. labor markets, leading to poorer pay and fewer benefits overall for American workers.[8]

What's more, no one is suggesting this massive importation of cheap labor has helped the low-income wage earner in America. In fact, even the most hard-core pro-immigration lobbyist never dares to suggest that an abundance of cheap labor helps the poor in America. In reality, this phenomenon increases the number of poor in our country. When surveys are conducted every year about Americans living in poverty, nearly 90 percent of those identified as living in poverty are noncitizens. So by giving them so many cheap employment opportunities, all we are doing is exploiting them and keeping them in poverty.

The fact is, we have a supply-and-demand problem. The supply problem is coming across the border. The demand side is the job magnet created by U.S. employers providing jobs for people who enter the country illegally. This imbalance has been allowed to proliferate because Congress and to some extent the White House have been unresponsive to the pleas of its constituents. Instead, Congress prefers to do the bidding of corporate special interests. With that in mind, I challenge any politician who rejects controlling our borders in order to "protect the economy" to consider this: there is no job that we can create in which foreigners cannot compete. But if we continue to import labor to do jobs inside the United States—jobs in the service sector, construction, etc.—while outsourcing jobs that do not require a physical presence in our country, there will be negative ramifications. Something bad is going to happen to the United States as a result of this job rigging. I suggest that, at a minimum, we will experience wage stagnation and declining wages. At worst, the ruling class will experience a worker revolt, the kind that America has never seen before.

Whoever in Congress and the White House believes they can live with that should be forced to warn their constituents to get ready for wage reductions, a major decline in the standard of living, and massive job losses—even as corporations earn record profits—because they are committed to the concept of free trade, which includes the free trade of labor. I'm betting not many congressmen and women would accept this challenge.

Washington's failure to control the nation's borders not only has a painful impact on workers at the bottom of the ladder but also on those increasingly farther up the income scale. The system holds down the pay of American workers and rewards illegals and the businesses that hire them. It breeds anger and resentment among citizens who cannot understand why illegal aliens receive government-funded health care, education benefits, and subsidized housing. In border communities, the masses of incoming illegals lay waste to the landscape and create a costly burden for agencies trying to keep public order. Moreover, the system makes a mockery of the U.S. tradition of encouraging legal immigration.

There is no such thing as a job an American will not take. It is just a matter of how much one is willing to pay to get the worker. As long as we continue to import cheap labor, the market economy will frustrate our desire to actually provide a good job for Americans. Instead, they will argue that the better option is to have cheaper products coming into our stores (even though it does require someone to buy those products). We cannot have a two-tiered economy of most people living at the lowest level while others live at the highest. Our future sharply comes into focus when we think about this kind of chaotic world—a world with infinite ingress into the United States.

In tandem with the lie that cheap labor is universally good for our country is the lie that illegal immigrants provide only economic benefits to America. The perpetrators of this fallacy assert that massive amounts of illegal aliens are an economic boon because they provide inexpensive services, pay lots of taxes, and purchase consumer goods. In truth, mass illegal immigration and so-called cheap labor is a lose-lose situation for U.S. taxpayers. When all taxes are paid and all costs are considered, illegal households created a net fiscal deficit of ten billion dollars in 2002.[9] Among the largest costs are Medicaid ($2.5 billion); treatment for the uninsured ($2.2 billion); food assistance programs such as food stamps, free school lunches, and the Women, Infant, and Children (WIC) nutrition plan ($1.9 billion); the federal prison and court systems ($1.6 billion); and federal aid to schools ($1.4 billion).[10]

And what about all of the services Americans have lost or are on the verge of losing because of the abuse heaped on them by massive migration? I frequently hear about local and regional hospitals that have closed, or are closing, because they are required to provide free medical treatment to illegals. What happens to the citizens who formerly benefited from them? Where will they go?

We are providing so much for millions of people who are giving back so little. There is so much more to this cost-benefit-economy equation than just the bottom lines of our major corporations.

15

The Threat to Our Health System by Illegal Immigration

The influx of illegal aliens has serious hidden medical consequences. We judge reality primarily by what we see. But what we do not see can be more dangerous, more expensive, and more deadly than what is seen.

—Madeleine Pelner Cosman, PhD

As I MENTIONED IN the previous chapter, Americans are finding it more and more difficult to obtain the services they need. The health-care industry is beginning to crumble under the intense costs that illegal aliens impose on our system. Known for its first-class health care, U.S. hospital and medical facilities are becoming second rate due to the benefits provided to illegal aliens while the country's citizens are denied treatment.

In February 2006 the federal government announced that, over the next decade, one dollar of every five dollars spent in the United States, would go toward health care. The Centers for Medicare and Medicaid Services projected that increased spending on hospital care, home-health services, drugs, and public-health programs will push total health-care spending from its current 16.2 percent of the economy to 20 percent in 2015.

The cost of providing free health care for illegal immigrants is one of the primary reasons the price of U.S. health care continues to rise. As in education, the price tag is astronomical and getting more expensive every year. Unless immigration laws change, the costs will only soar.

One reason Americans pay so much to care for illegal aliens is a federal law that prohibits hospitals from turning away any patients—whether legal citizen or not—due to their inability to pay. The Emergency Medical Treatment and Active Labor Act (EMTALA), an unfunded government mandate, declares that every emergency department at every hospital must treat all patients who arrive with an "emergency." According to EMTALA, an emergency can consist of a cough, headache, hangnail, cardiac arrest, herniated lumbar disc, drug addiction, alcohol overdose, gunshot wound, automobile trauma, HIV-positive infection, or mental or personality disorders.[1] That means anyone who comes to a hospital emergency department must be treated to the best of that hospital's technological ability or transferred, if needed, to a more capable facility, even if the patient doesn't have a thin dime to his or her name. Not that that isn't a compassionate and logical policy for Americans, mind you. The problem is that the law is abused by illegal aliens who specifically come to the United States to obtain health care. In fact, Mexican government documents provide details about this law and describe it as a benefit available to its citizens who travel illegally to the United States. EMTALA also prevents U.S. health-care workers and hospital officials from inquiring about a patient's legal status.

There is little argument among experts and the paying public that America's health-care system is already in crisis. Health-insurance premiums are skyrocketing, as are costs for medical treatment and prescription medications. Add the cost of massive numbers of illegal immigrants, and U.S. taxpayers are literally on the hook for tens of billions of dollars annually—even when hospitals get reimbursed for providing free migrant care. Because illegals bleed so much money and so many resources from hospitals—especially those in the border regions—many of these facilities have had to shutter their emergency departments or close entirely. By spring 2005 eighty-four California hospitals had either declared bankruptcy or were closing because they were losing too much money due to indigent illegal migrant care.[2] The Los Angeles County Trauma Care Network, renowned for its emergency medical services, lost many of its twenty-two hospitals and emergency physicians and surgeons due to financial losses as a direct result of EMTALA.[3]

Medical lawyer Madeleine Pelner Cosman revealed in her report "Illegal Aliens and American Medicine" that violence by illegal immigrants served as one of the largest causes of financial loss to emergency departments around the country.

> Illegal aliens perpetrate much violent crime, the results of which arrive at EDs. "Dump and run" patients, often requiring tracheotomy or thoracotomy for stab or gunshot wounds, are dropped on the hospital sidewalk or at the ED as the car speeds away. Usually such incidents are connected to drugs and gangs. Even if the hospital is not exclusively dedicated to trauma care, EMTALA still governs treatment.
>
> While most people coming to EDs throughout the United States are not poor and have medical insurance, cities such as Los Angeles with large illegal alien populations, high crime, and powerful immigrant gangs are losing their hospitals to the ravages of unpaid care under EMTALA.

Meanwhile, some forty-three million Americans are without adequate health insurance. While they too have a right to emergency medical treatment, the law doesn't mandate government payment for that care. Even many Americans with health insurance in immigrant-heavy regions of the country have complained that their care is vastly delayed or even unavailable because health-care facilities have far too many illegal migrants to treat.

It's nearly impossible to gauge the cost of providing free health care to illegal migrants, but it is safe to say it is in the billions of dollars. The cost doesn't only come in terms of finance; Americans are paying for it in terms of exposure to increased diseases.

In her spring 2005 report "The Seen and the Unseen," Cosman revealed "many illegal aliens harbor fatal diseases that American medicine fought and vanquished long ago, such as drug-resistant tuberculosis, malaria, leprosy, plague, polio, dengue, and Chagas disease." According to the report, "[Tuberculosis] had largely disappeared from America, thanks to excellent hygiene and powerful modern drugs such as isoniazid and rifampin. TB's swift, deadly return is lethal for nearly 60 percent of those infected because of the new Multi-Drug Resistant Tuberculosis. Until recently, MDR-TB was endemic to Mexico."

Other health threats posed by illegal immigration include:

- Chagas disease (also called American trypanosomiasis or the "kissing bug disease") is transmitted by the reduviid bug, which prefers to bite the lips and face. The protozoan parasite that it carries, Trypanosoma cruzi, infects eighteen million people annually in Latin America and causes fifty thousand deaths. The disease also infiltrates America's blood supply. Chagas affects blood transfusions and transplanted organs. No cure exists. Hundreds of blood recipients may be silently infected.
- Leprosy (also known as Hansen's disease) was so rare in America that in forty years only nine hundred people were afflicted. Suddenly, in the past three years, America has more than seven thousand cases of leprosy. Leprosy now is endemic to the Northeastern states because illegal aliens and other immigrants brought leprosy from Brazil, the Caribbean, India, and Mexico.
- Dengue fever is exceptionally rare in America, though common in Bangladesh, Ecuador, Malaysia, Mexico, Peru, Thailand, and Vietnam. Recently, there was a virulent outbreak of dengue fever in Webb County, Texas, which borders Mexico. Though dengue is usually not a fatal disease, dengue hemorrhagic fever routinely kills.
- Polio was eradicated in America but now reappears in illegal immigrants, as do intestinal parasites.
- Malaria was obliterated, but is now reemerging in Texas.[4]

These are diseases that all Americans were vaccinated against decades ago. As a result, all of them were eradicated from the United States. Now, strains of these viruses and diseases have mutated into forms that modern medicine cannot currently treat.

ANCHOR BABIES, AWEIGH!

ONE REASON for the rise in the number of occurrences of these diseases can be attributed to the so-called anchor baby phenomenon. By simply being born in the United States, a child automatically becomes an American citizen eligible for a range of welfare and public-assistance benefits. Mexican mothers frequently come to the United States just to give birth. Ambulances from Mexico routinely bring patients to American hospitals because they are aware of the U.S. treatment mandate.[5]

Most Americans don't realize it (thanks to their multicultural education), but a little-discussed constitutional provision actually allows all of this to happen legally through what's called birthright citizenship. Though the provision was not authored with the intent of granting automatic citizenship to children of persons in the country illegally, courts throughout the years have held that it does.

The first sentence of the Fourteenth Amendment says, "All persons born or naturalized in the United States, and subject to the jurisdiction thereof, are citizens of the United States and of the state wherein they reside." Written and passed in the immediate aftermath of the Civil War, the law's intent was to prevent states from denying citizenship to newly freed slaves. In 1866 Sen. Jacob Howard, coauthor of the citizenship clause of the amendment, said, "Every person born within the limits of the United States, and subject to their jurisdiction, is by virtue of natural law and national law a citizen of the United States. *This will not, of course, include persons born in the United States who are foreigners, aliens, who belong to the families of ambassadors or foreign ministers accredited to the Government of the United States, but will include every other class of persons* (emphasis added)."[6] Jacobs's explanation seems very clear, but many of today's judges have rendered their own interpretation of the amendment, making the provision exactly the opposite of its original intent.

As such, a loophole has been created in the law, and it has become so well known abroad that aliens near and far exploit it to the tune of billions of dollars every year. The tens of thousands of children born to illegal aliens are called "anchor babies" because once they are born in the United States, they serve as an anchor to keep themselves and their families firmly (and legally) in the country. Once born, these children immediately qualify for a huge number of federal, state, and local benefit programs.

In my work as chairman of the House Immigration Reform Caucus,

I have traveled frequently throughout the Southwest where this problem is the worst. I have witnessed scores of Mexican women come to the border just to wait until they go into labor. They then ask to be rushed, not to a Mexican hospital, but to an American maternity ward. Hospitals near the border say illegal immigrant women who are near term in their pregnancies actually sit in their cars in the parking lot, waiting to go into labor, so they can walk into an emergency room and be admitted for immediate maternal care.

In the instances where undocumented migrant women arrive at established U.S. border crossings, border agents—instead of turning them back—admit them. When I asked a Customs official about this, he said, "We are not medical people. We don't have that kind of expertise. We don't know. Somebody says they are sick, we wave them on in." If you spend any time near these ports of entry, you will see Mexican ambulances drive up and demand the Customs agents let them through because they claim to have critically ill patients on board and need immediate passage. Consequently, U.S. officials wave through these foreign ambulances. The Mexican government, incidentally, distributes pamphlets and other information that describe the free medical services north of the border. One estimate puts the number of children born to illegal aliens in the United States at three hundred thousand annually:[7]

Cristobal Silverio emigrated illegally from Mexico to Stockton, Calif., in 1997 to work as a fruit picker. He brought with him his wife, Felipa, and three children, 19, 12 and 8—all illegals. When Felipa gave birth to her fourth child, daughter Flor, the family had what is referred to as an "anchor baby"—an American citizen by birth who provided the entire Silverio clan a ticket to remain in the U.S. permanently. But Flor was born premature, spent three months in the neonatal incubator and cost the San Joaquin Hospital more than $300,000. Meanwhile, oldest daughter Lourdes married an illegal alien and gave birth to a daughter, too. Her name is Esmeralda. And Felipa had yet another child, Cristian. The two Silverio anchor babies generate $1,000 per month in public welfare funding for the family. Flor gets $600 a month for asthma. Healthy Cristian gets $400. While the Silverios earned $18,000 last year picking fruit, they picked up another $12,000 for their two "anchor babies."[8]

The anchor baby dilemma was laid bare in testimony before the House Judiciary Committee's Subcommittee on Immigration, Border Security, and Claims in September 2005, when John C. Eastman, professor at Chapman University School of Law and director of the Claremont Institute Center for Constitutional Jurisprudence, gave a clear example of how dangerous the loophole can be:

At 4:05 p.m. on the afternoon of September 26, 1980—day 327 of the Iranian hostage crisis—Nadiah Hussen Hamdi, born Nadia Hussen Fattah in Taif, Saudi Arabia, gave birth to a son, Yaser Esam Hamdi, at the Women's Hospital in Baton Rouge, Louisiana. I mention the Iranian hostage crisis because Yaser Hamdi might just as easily have been the son of parents of Iran, then in a hostile standoff with the United States, as of Saudi Arabia. The boy's father, Esam Fouad Hamdi, a native of Mecca, Saudi Arabia and still a Saudi citizen, was residing at the time in Baton Rouge on a temporary visa to work as a chemical engineer on a project for Exxon. While the boy was still a toddler, the Hamdi family returned to its native Saudi Arabia, and for the next twenty years Yaser Esam Hamdi would not set foot again on American soil. . . . Yaser Hamdi's path after coming of age would instead take him to the hills of Afghanistan, to take up with the Taliban (and perhaps the al-Qaeda terrorist organization it harbored) in its war against the forces of the Northern Alliance and, ultimately, against the armed forces of the United States as well. In late 2001, during a battle near Konduz, Afghanistan between Northern Alliance forces and the Taliban unit in which Hamdi was serving and while armed with a Kalashnikov AK-47 military assault rifle, Hamdi surrendered to the Northern Alliance forces and was taken by them to a military prison in Mazar-e-Sharif, Afghanistan. From there Hamdi was transferred to Sheberghan, Afghanistan, where he was interrogated by a U.S. interrogation team, determined to be an enemy combatant, and eventually transferred to U.S. control, first in Kandahar, Afghanistan and then at the U.S. Naval Base in Guantanamo Bay, Cuba. . . . Unlike his fellow enemy combatants being detained in Guantanamo Bay, Hamdi had a get-out-of-Cuba-free card. When U.S. officials learned that Hamdi had been born in Louisiana, they transferred Hamdi (free of charge!) to the Naval Brig in Norfolk, Virginia, from where Hamdi, under the auspices of his father acting as his next-friend, has waged a legal battle seeking access to attorneys and a writ of habeas corpus compelling his release. This, because under the generally-accepted interpretation of the Fourteenth Amendment's citizenship clause, Hamdi's birth to Saudi parents who were temporarily visiting one of the United States as the time of his birth made him a U.S. citizen, entitled to the full panoply of rights that the U.S. Constitution guarantees to U.S. citizens. Hamdi petitioned the federal district court in Virginia for a writ of habeas corpus, seeking to challenge his detention. His case was ultimately heard by the Supreme Court of the United States, which held, in an opinion by Justice [Sandra Day] O'Connor, that Hamdi had a Due Process right to challenge the factual basis for his classification and detention as an enemy combatant.[9]

This is an outrage and should never have happened. America, however, is one of the few countries, maybe the only country in the world, that has such birthright-citizenship laws.

"Yaser Hamdi's case has highlighted for us all the dangers of recognizing unilateral claims of birthright citizenship by the children of people only temporarily visiting this country, and highlighted even more the dangers of recognizing such claims by the children of those who have arrived illegally to do us harm," Eastman said. He added that Congress needed to reassert its authority and make clear, by resolution, "its view that the 'subject to the jurisdiction' phrase of the Citizenship Clause has meaning of fundamental importance to the naturalization policy of the nation."[10]

Other countries have recognized similar problems and loopholes in their laws and have fixed them. In January 2003 the Irish Supreme Court handed down a landmark ruling that declared the immigrant parents of an Irish-born child could be deported. The ruling was the first reversal of Ireland's very liberal policy of granting residency and citizenship to anyone who came to the country and had a baby. Then, in June 2004, the people of Ireland nullified birthright citizenship with the approval of the twenty-seventh amendment of the Irish Constitution. It reads: "Notwithstanding any other provision, a person born on the island of Ireland who does not have at the time of birth of that person at least one parent who is an Irish citizen or entitled to be an Irish citizen is not entitled to Irish citizenship or nationality unless provided by law." America should follow Ireland's lead and eliminate a huge incentive that lures illegal aliens to our country.

CRAG: A PROPOSAL TO RECLAIM AMERICA'S HOSPITALS AND SLOW ILLEGAL IMMIGRATION

MADELEINE PELNER COSMAN'S report about illegal immigration and its effect on our health-care system did more than point out the obvious problems that are crippling hospitals across the country. Cosman closed her report with a call to action known as "CRAG: four critical actions to reclaim American's EDs; to restore medicine's proud scientific excellence and profitability; and to protect Americans against bacterial, viral, parasitic, and fungal infectious diseases that illegal aliens carry across our borders." In her commonsense immigration plan, she proposes the following:

- *Close America's Borders:* Prevent illegal entry with fences. . . . Deport illegal aliens.
- *Rescind the Citizenship of Anchor Babies:* Gravid wombs should not guarantee free medical care and instant infant citizenship in America. We must reestablish the original limits on citizenship, and remove incentives for indigent Mexicans and others to break America's immigration law.
- *Aiding and Abetting Illegal Aliens Is a Crime:* Punish it. This will anger devotees of illegal aliens who believe that the Constitution guarantees them civil rights.
- *Grant No New Amnesties:* Fighting against illegal aliens is fighting for individualistic America: land of moral strength, and home of responsible liberty.[11]

Cosman ends her report with the simple line: "As we fight to reclaim medicine, so we defend our nation." She has embarked on a philosophy that should pervade every service, business, and profession in our country. If we refuse to take a no-nonsense approach to illegal immigration, we must face the fact that an amicable illegal-alien policy will put us on the path to becoming a third-world country all too soon.

16

Environmental Impact from Illegal Immigration

[Illegal immigrants] turn the land into a vast latrine, leaving behind revolting mounds of personal refuse and enough discarded plastic bags to stock a Wal-Mart.

—Donald L. Barlett and James B. Steele, "Who Left the Door Open?" *Time* magazine, September 20, 2004

GEORGE AND LINDA MORIN own and manage a cattle ranch of twelve thousand acres situated four miles from the Arizona-Mexico border. For years, they have witnessed people coming across the border looking for jobs—people whom they befriended and aided economically. This was never a problem for them until the last ten or fifteen years.

Then the Morins began to notice a steady increase in the number of illegal aliens coming across their land. Over the past five or six years, this flow has become, as they put it, a flood. Their large cattle ranch is a family business requiring a lot of very hard work. Drought, diseases, and volatile market crashes for beef cattle have made cattle ranching a tough business in even the best of circumstances. The massive flood of illegal immigration has added more hardships. Consider the following: the water lines that carry water to the cattle have been cut or broken so many times that the Morins have lost count. Water in this part of the country is, of course, very valuable and something ranchers are dependent upon for their existence. For reasons that are sometimes difficult to explain, illegal immigrants often vandalize these water lines and the wells, even though many ranchers will leave out cups so they can drink from the well.

The same thing goes for fencing. Repairing cut fences is now a routine task. While in Arizona, I witnessed hundreds of miles of broken fences along the border. Electric switches for water pumps were often jammed or vandalized. The Morin ranch lost numerous cattle that died after eating plastic trash bags dropped by trespassers as they passed through the land. This sight is all too common throughout this area. There are regions of the Southwest, especially in southern Arizona, that are referred to as "pickup sites." These are places where large numbers of illegal aliens gather to get a ride because it is near a road or highway.

When illegals gather at the pickup sites, they embark on the next part of the journey. They discard everything they have been carrying because the "coyotes" (the people who help bring the illegals into the United States) require extra space in their trucks. When I have walked through these sites, I have seen large garbage dumps. I have referred to the Organ Pipe Cactus National Monument as the Organ Pipe Cactus National Dump because of the way it appears now. The trash left behind by the trespassers is not only dangerous to the cattle that eat it, it is despoiling the land and environment in numerous ways. In one day, George Morin collected forty-two syringes and discarded drug containers left by one group.

And all of this occurs in plain sight. An incredible outcry would erupt if the media were to pay any attention to it. In fact, I continuously wonder why there is no uproar from groups like the Sierra Club, Friends of the Earth, and other environmental groups that often publicly deplore the despoiling of the land. Instead, these groups seldom say a word about this problem because it is connected with illegal immigration and, therefore, not a topic to be discussed by left-wing organizations.

People coming into this country illegally have essentially destroyed large chunks of our pristine desert along the southern border. Millions upon millions of feet walking have created thousands of footpaths that cannot be regenerated by the natural environment. In 2002 nearly ninety-two thousand acres of the Coronado National Forest near Tucson, Arizona, were lost to forest fires. In a report by Gale Achenbrenner, public affairs officer at the Coronado National Forest, "Warming and cooking fires built and abandoned by undocumented aliens have caused wildfires that have destroyed natural and cultural resources."

Where plants are threatened and destroyed, so is wildlife. In 2004, Californians for Population Stabilization (CAPS) revealed that "99 percent of its native grassland, 80 percent of its coastal wetlands and at least 73 plants and animals are extinct in our state. Over 150 animals and 280 plants are listed as endangered, threatened, rare." Diana Hull, president of CAPS, argued that the prevention of environment degradation is impossible to stop "until we stabilize our population. California also faces water and energy shortages, but politicians lack the courage and the will to tackle the problem."

Hull's statement points to another serious problem threatening not just the landscape of the border states but the rest of the nation's natural resources. By allowing millions of people into the country, the increase in the consumption of natural resources leaves an ever-decreasing supply of those resources.

According to the Census Bureau, of the 281 million people in the United States in 2000, 31 million were naturalized citizens, resident legal aliens, and resident illegal aliens.[1] By the year 2100, the Census Bureau projects that the population will increase by 50 percent with 66 percent of the population consisting of post-2000 immigrants and their families.[2] With this kind of projected growth, there are certain aspects of the environment that are sure to be impacted. Consider the following:

- One acre of natural habitat or farmland is converted to built-up space or highway for each person added to the U.S. population.
- More than 99.3 percent of U.S. food comes from the land.
- Of the nearly 470 million acres of arable land that are now in cultivation in the United States, more than 1 million acres are lost from cultivation each year due to urbanization, multiplying transportation networks, and industrial expansion.
- If present population growth and other trends continue, over the next sixty years, both degradation and urbanization will diminish our arable land base of 470 million acres by 120 million acres.
- Only 0.6 percent of arable land per person will be available in 2050, whereas more than 1.2 acres per person are needed to

provide a diverse diet (currently 1.6 acres of arable land per person are available).

- A doubling of the American population will accelerate the need for food. For every 1 percent increase in food demand, the price at the farm gate increases 4.5 percent.
- If present trends in population growth, domestic food consumption, and topsoil loss continue, the U.S. food exports (and the income from them) will cease by 2030.
- Groundwater provides 31 percent of the water used in U.S. agriculture and is, on average, being depleted 25 percent in excess of recharge rates.
- Even if water management is substantially improved, the 560 million Americans by 2060 will have only 700 gallons per day per capita, considered a minimum for all human needs. This assumes even distribution, which is not the case—much of our population and agricultural production is in arid and semi-arid regions.[3]

Thus, conserving our resources is not enough. We must do everything possible to secure our borders and stabilize our population. One such measure is to propose legislation that promotes "carrying capacity." This concept:

> refers to the number of individuals who can be supported in a given area within natural resource limits, and without degrading the natural social, cultural and economic environment for present and future generations. The carrying capacity for any given area is not fixed. It can be altered by improved technology, but mostly it is changed for the worse by pressures that accompany a population increase. As the environment is degraded, carrying capacity actually shrinks, leaving the environment no longer able to support even the number of people who could formerly have lived in the area on a sustainable basis.[4]

By proposing legislation that promotes carrying capacity, we tackle several problems, including environmental issues, immigration reform, and national security.

Perhaps the most disconcerting aspect is the social environment that residents and children on the border are facing. There are more dangerous aspects than human waste and unsightly trash polluting the landscape. Because many of the people coming across the border are carrying large quantities of illegal drugs for resale, guards with automatic weapons accompany them. These are not people who simply drop everything and run when they are confronted by a rancher or a Border Patrol official. They opt to open fire, and many times have done just that.

Some of the illegals who are not directly connected to drug trafficking have been very indifferent, very aggressive, and very antagonistic to the ranchers in the area. Ranchers have been threatened physically, assaulted, family members threatened, had their wells vandalized, or endured break-ins at their homes, barns, or outbuildings. And so almost everyone in this area is armed. Children go to school armed because their parents are afraid to send them alone.

Ranchers are forced to keep shotguns or other firearms by their doors. And they do this out of necessity, not because they're gun freaks. As one rancher told me, "Nobody should have to live like this. We have lived here for generations. Nobody ever locked their doors. Nobody ever locked their cars." This was the idyllic, picturesque rural life that most people believed existed in this country. Yet another aspect of the American way of life is threatened by these open-border policies.

Larry and Toni Vance live just one mile from the border and three miles from the Douglas, Arizona, port of entry. Larry is the son of a legal Mexican immigrant. The couple has lived in the area for twenty-nine years. Like other American families who have been born and raised along the border, the Vance family has seen many changes over the last three decades. And they have seen a change for the worse in the illegal aliens crossing their land.

In the 1970s and 1980s, there were few drug smugglers. Most groups coming across their land were small (numbering three to five people), and the migrants were polite and often stopped to ask directions or for a drink of water. Still, there were times when bandits posed a danger to the border residents. Burglaries were common; the Vance home was burglarized twice. Eventually there was a crackdown on the border crossings. The Border Patrol was beefed up, and the crime problem was brought under control.

But by the mid-1990s, the Vances noticed a dramatic increase in the number of groups of illegal trespassers. By 1997 the Vance family witnessed about twenty groups of twenty or more people a day, and those groups would pass through at all hours of the day and night.

The makeup of the groups also began to change. Now women and children, sometimes even pregnant women and elderly people, were part of the growing groups. At one point the illegals were coming so close to the Vance house, the couple could not sleep at night because their dogs would bark themselves hoarse each night at all the foot traffic.

In September 1999 the Vances' two dogs were poisoned. Bandits preyed on the helpless illegal aliens, robbing, beating, and raping the migrants. The screams of the victims were often heard across the desert at night. The Vances installed a high chain-link fence around their house and wrought-iron window guards. Such measures were unheard-of in rural Arizona until the mid-1990s; such changes are traceable to the rising crime rate from illegal aliens.

The Vances' horses often escaped and had to be chased the next day because their fences were knocked down or cut. By 2000 Larry Vance stopped trying to keep horses because it became too difficult and too expensive to keep the fences repaired.

Like other ranchers, Larry used to keep water troughs filled for the wildlife. But he can no longer do that because illegal aliens constantly break his water lines. Additionally, the Vances have to contend with huge amounts of trash left by the migrant flocks.

Traffic accidents caused by illegal aliens chasing other vehicles or just careening into a ditch have become regular occurrences. Many local residents have been killed by crashing into cars and trucks driven by rampaging illegals as they race across the border.

The lives of ranchers like Larry and Toni Vance and George and Linda Morin have been radically altered in the last decade because their own government has repeatedly failed to protect them and their land from invasion. And *invasion* is exactly the proper term for what's occurring.

Not many people beyond their immediate family and the immediate area around Douglas know of the Vances' predicament. But all Americans should know that these people are in a war zone. They are fighting a war, and they feel like their own government has abandoned them.

When I visited them, I did not bring them good news. I could not say to them, "Don't worry, the government is going to come to your rescue. The government is going to do what it knows it should do and what it promises to do for every American citizen, namely, to protect your lives and property." I wish I could have told them that. But in all candor, I couldn't. That's because this government has chosen to ignore the Vances, the Morins, and all the families who are living along our borders.

I have never seen a greater divide between what the people of this country want and need and what their elected officials are willing to give them. The time to act is now. If we don't, the dire scenarios cataloged at the beginning of this chapter will quickly become a grievous reality for all Americans.

PART 3

What Needs to Be Done

17

Steps for Reform

I FIRMLY BELIEVE THAT we must reaffirm the principles of citizenship and of American identity if we are to survive as a free people in the twenty-first century. This comes not from a fear of immigration. As a son of immigrants, I welcome and support immigration. What worries me is that the nation our new immigrants seek to find at the end of their journey may not be the nation of their dreams and grand ambitions. If we are to remain true to our history, we must also remain true to our destiny. Our destiny is not to be a vague, confusing collection of ethnic groups or religious sects, but rather it is a continuation of the land of freedom and opportunity, the world's beacon of hope for all who are oppressed.

To rekindle that desire and remain focused on that destiny, we must renew the bonds of citizenship and the values and institutions that nourish and sustain those bonds. The ideology of multiculturalism does not understand this. In fact, the multicultural movement is at war with every idea of America as has been understood for more than two hundred years.

I hope and pray that most Americans understand this and will do everything in their power to ensure our success. With the help of the good people of this nation, we will prevail. But we have to be willing to confront this issue, no matter how uncomfortable it is for us to talk about it and no matter how challenging it is to overcome.

It is undeniable that massive immigration combined with the multi-cultural philosophy in this country has huge ramifications. Some may believe those ramifications are positive; I believe they are negative.

I believe that the leadership of this nation must begin a dialogue with America. When I say dialogue, I mean renewing a commitment to the idea of America on the part of all the people who come to positions of authority and responsibility. Is Western civilization, as epitomized by the American experience, worth saving? This is the question we must pose. And to answer it correctly, we have to have all information available to us.

We have to teach our children about the nation's value as well as highlight its warts. It is important that we not gloss over the inequities, that we not discard from our text any discussion of slavery or any of the issues we know to be negative in our history. They have to be discussed and understood in order to be overcome. Additionally, we must discuss the factual positive elements of Western civilization and what it has brought to the world. Why is that so scary to the academic community, to the media, and to pop culture? Why is it so comfortable for members of the pop culture and the people in television and in the movies to stand up and criticize—only criticize—what it is to be an American when they reap so many benefits from being American themselves? How hypocritical. But how comfortable and profitable it is for them to do so, and how easy it is for them to do so.

Shortly after 9/11, when Congress was engaged in a debate over the possibility of a conflict in the Middle East and the efficacy of that conflict—whether or not it was in the national interests of the United States to embark upon this venture, whether a preemptive strike by the United States was justified, and whether or not sending men and women into harm's way was appropriate—I took the House floor to quote from some speeches made at "pro-peace rallies" in Washington DC. I said the press likely misidentified these speeches as "pro-peace," just as the media had misidentified the rallies I attended and spoke at as "pro-war." Most of the discussions and most of the people exhorting the crowd were not really interested in the concept of peace and the need for it but talked instead about the problems with America and saying that America needed its own "regime change." That America needed another "revolution." They also led chants of *Allah Akbar, Allah Akbar,* at these rallies.

Many in the crowds of these "pro-peace" rallies were Hollywood actors and actresses. I was intrigued by the attention given to these entertainment celebrities. In one radio report, an actor shared his opinions about the war. He was, of course, very critical of the United States and our actions. I have no qualm with this actor. He has every right to express his opinions, as does a postman, a waitress, any citizen of this country. What I found interesting, however, was the attention paid to that particular point of view by these people who, admittedly, have no particular expertise.

After 9/11, a friend was getting into a cab. He saw on the front seat a newspaper report about former President Clinton's speech in which he said he linked the 9/11 attacks with America's treatment of Native Americans in the past and the history of slavery.

My friend said to the driver, "I see you read about President Clinton's speech. What did you think of it?"

The cab driver replied, "I thought it was baloney." He said of the terrorists, "These people do not hate us for what we have done wrong; they hate us for what we do *right.*"

What an interesting and profound observation. The cab driver said that we do things right. We help people. We have such freedoms in the United States—freedom of speech and the press, freedom of religion, freedom of the sexes to vote and to share the rights afforded to all citizens—so many rights that are not recognized in the countries from which the 9/11 hijackers came.

Now, a little story such as that found no play in the national media at the time of the "pro-peace" and "pro-war" rallies. Perhaps there was no reason to report it because, after all, this was a Washington DC cab driver. What was his expertise? He talks to a lot of people, but he's not really a person we should listen to because of his great acumen and experience.

Yet, interestingly, the press pays a great deal of attention to people in the media and the entertainment world who come forward with their pronouncements about what is right in terms of our foreign policy and what is wrong. They turn to actors like Sean Penn and actresses like

Susan Sarandon (although she does not want to be called an "actress" because that distinguishes a gender difference). These people are given a lot of attention and tremendous airtime. People listen to them and say, "Wow. That is how they feel."

I am intrigued by it because they are all, without exception, extremely liberal and, as such, are opposed to any U.S. military action in either Afghanistan or Iraq. Ironically, I don't remember anybody condemning President Clinton for tossing missiles around when he felt they were appropriate. I don't recall any of them complaining about his pursuit of a war in Yugoslavia that was against a country posing absolutely no threat to the United States. No one ever suggested that former Yugoslavian president Slobodan Milosevic was a threat to this country. He was a horrible national leader, no doubt, but he posed no danger to the United States. Yet we carried out a war against him, and all of today's outspoken critics of American foreign action were silent.

During this war against the murderous Saddam Hussein, I have heard these high-profile celebrities constantly rail against the United States because we deposed him and wiped out the terrorists we believe he was sponsoring. I suggest these "stars" have absolutely no more grasp of this issue than the cab driver in Washington DC. I happen to agree with the cab driver's interpretation, but I don't recall seeing him being interviewed on television. And yet, because of the many people that he sees during the course of a day in the nation's capital, he is more likely to be politically astute than anyone in Hollywood. But we don't talk about him because he is not a national figure—and, of course, because he has a different interpretation of events from that of the stereotypical left-wing anti-American sentiment that is expressed by the pop idols.

Yes, something has changed dramatically. The right-minded people who exist in that medium are afraid to express the cabbie's sentiments for fear their peers will shun them. What has happened that has allowed this to occur? I suggest that it's time to regenerate a discussion of American principles and ideas; to help everybody—our children and adults—understand the importance of those ideas and ideals; to expect the immigrants coming to this country to have a burning desire to be Americans, and that to come here for any other reason is not acceptable. To come here simply for economic gain and to hold allegiance to other countries politically, ethnically, and linguistically is not acceptable.

It is not acceptable because this "nonallegiant" attitude is cancerous; it will sap the strength of America. Such a cancer will destroy our ability to be successful in the ongoing clash of civilizations. It will lead to our demise.

For that reason in December 2005, as chairman of the Immigration Reform Caucus, I sent a letter to House majority leader Roy Blunt and Rules Committee chairman David Dreier sounding the alarm to fix our broken immigration system. I wrote:

> Our border crisis is multifaceted—it has created problems on many policy fronts that one would not think pertain to immigration. For each problem Members will want to propose a solution, and as a courtesy to you, I have listed some of these proposals from my colleagues on the House Immigration Reform Caucus below.

FIXING OUR BROKEN BORDERS

Begin Building a Border Security Fence
- Put troops on the border
- End "catch and release"
- Mandate passport usage for everyone traveling internationally
- Make volunteer border patrol a sanctioned federal activity
- Suspend visa waiver program

Enforcing the Law Throughout the Country
- Require a federal response when local law enforcement asks to have illegal aliens arrested
- Restrict federal money that goes to local governments that have illegal alien sanctuary policies
- Close the loophole that allows religious organizations and their agents to be immune from illegal-alien-harboring laws
- Make DUI a deportable offense
- Increase penalties for the smuggling of illegal aliens
- Increase penalties for terrorists who are illegal aliens

- Increase penalties for gang members who are illegal aliens
- Draft minimum standards for birth certificates and birth/death registries
- Make unlawful presence in the United States a felony

Stopping Businesses from Hiring Illegals

- Make employment verification mandatory
- Eliminate the business tax write-off for illegal workers
- Increase the penalty for employers who hire illegal aliens
- Make businesses that hire illegal aliens ineligible for future guest workers

Reducing the Incentive to Come Illegally

- Disallow all federal funding for states that offer in-state tuition to illegal aliens
- Disallow the matricula consular card as a legal form of identification
- Reform the use of individual taxpayer identification numbers
- Eliminate Social Security totalization for illegal aliens

Disentangling Foreign Policy from Immigration

- Block any immigration provisions from trade bills
- Block visas to countries that refuse to take their nationals back
- Reduce the availability of yearly legal visas per country by the number of illegal aliens from such country

Restoring the Meaning of Citizenship

- End birthright citizenship for illegal aliens
- Eliminate dual citizenship
- Make English the official language
- Write the oath of citizenship into law
- Strengthen safeguards against voter fraud

Reforming Legal Immigration

- Eliminate the visa lottery
- Eliminate chain migration

- Eliminate H-1B visas [temporary work permits]
- Eliminate unskilled worker green cards
- Create a Department of Immigration or a cabinet-level agency

It has been nearly a decade since Congress rewrote the immigration law, and we are only now dealing with it again because we have a security crisis on our hands. Over the last decade, Americans have cried out to seal our porous borders and to enforce the law. We must seize this opportunity to accomplish real reform.

18

Preserving Our National Existence

> We've all felt a renewal of what it means to be citizens of the United States. It is also time for us to become citizens of the world.
>
> —Tom Regan, *Christian Science Monitor,*
> September 21, 2001

During a January 2006 debate, former Colorado senator Gary Hart said: "globalization is eroding national sovereignty."[1] Globalization, he said, had replaced *citizen* with *consumer* in the minds of many people. The United States isn't so much a country anymore, he implied, as it is a market.

The same thing is happening throughout the West. Since the Maastricht Treaty finalizing the European Union was adopted, Europeans have become citizens of a union rather than remain sovereign Dutch, German, etc., citizens. For many Europeans, their nation has simply become a place on the planet where they reside, no longer a part of their identity or a component of their culture.

Multicultural elites now frequently describe themselves as "citizens of the world." If given the chance, they would replace loyalty to any one country with loyalty to humanity, loyalty to Mother Earth, and—in some cases—loyalty to *them*. This rhetoric has trickled down to impressionable young people. Too frequently young people tell me that America is a continent, not a nation. Throughout the West there is now an outright assault on citizenship. Multiculturalism has advanced so much that it denigrates the value of a national birthright.

Jed Bartlett, the fictional president on the NBC television series *The West Wing*, lectured an adviser on the concept and importance of citizenship during an episode that featured a terrorist attack:

> Did you know that two thousand years ago, a Roman citizen could walk across the face of the known world free of the fear of molestation? He could walk across the earth unharmed, cloaked only in the protection of the words *Civis Romanus*: "I am a Roman citizen." So great was the retribution of Rome universally understood as certain should any harm befall even one of its citizens.

He was not only describing the power of Rome but the importance the empire placed on protecting its citizens. Rome respected its citizens and demanded that others do so too. For the Romans, citizenship was real.

The book of Acts in the Bible records that when soldiers prepared to flog the apostle Paul and discovered he was a Roman citizen, they immediately ceased their mistreatment of him. They were afraid that word would get out that they had begun to engage in injustice toward a citizen. The centurion told his superior, "Take heed what thou doest: for this man is a Roman."[2] This prompted the Roman authorities to take extraordinary measures to protect the dignity of their fellow citizen. When sending Paul to be judged, "He called unto him two centurions, saying, Make ready two hundred soldiers to go to Caesarea, and horsemen threescore and ten, and spearmen two hundred, at the third hour of the night; and provide them beasts, that they may set Paul on, and bring him safe unto Felix the governor."[3] These extraordinary precautions were taken to protect even an unpopular Roman citizen from a dangerous mob.

In a similar fashion, around the turn of the twentieth century, Theodore Roosevelt was willing to use the power of the American state to protect the dignity of its citizens. When Moroccan tribesmen kidnapped an American citizen, Ion Perdicaris, Roosevelt dispatched a naval fleet and cabled the Moroccan government, "We want either Perdicaris alive or [tribal warlord Ahmad Ibn Muhammad] Raisuli [who had captured Perdicaris] dead." The message was not lost on either the Moroccan sultan or the warlord Raisuli.[4] The U.S. president was willing to go to great lengths to protect the dignity of a *single* American. Perdicaris safely returned home.

When Mexican revolutionary Pancho Villa attacked Columbus, New Mexico, on March 9, 1916, President Woodrow Wilson responded by sending twelve thousand troops under Gen. John "Black Jack" Pershing to apprehend him. Pershing's expedition delved deep into Mexico, and although it was ultimately unsuccessful, the fact that Wilson ordered the reprisal was noteworthy.

In today's world, by contrast, Americans traveling abroad are encouraged to conceal their citizenship. They are concerned about becoming the targets of attacks while visiting foreign countries.

Unlike Roosevelt or Wilson, when the World Trade Center was first bombed on February 26, 1993, America did nothing. As to our southern neighbor, drug-corrupted Mexican troops and police frequently make armed incursions into the United States engaging U.S. authorities in chases and gun battles. As was mentioned earlier, the United States has suffered more than two hundred such incursions since 1997. As a result, I have written the president of Mexico. I have written the secretary of state of the United States. I have asked our administration what it intends to do about this. Periodically, I am told that our diplomats "intend to bring it up at the highest levels of government." In layman's terms, that means, "We will do nothing."

Therein lies the difference a century makes. The greatest threat to our nation today does not come from invasion by foreign soldiers but rather from internal decay, a loss of identity, and a de-emphasis on the value of American citizenship.

Americans are rapidly approaching a point in our history where we will have to ask ourselves some telling questions. What is the value of the nation-state? Does it have merit? Without the nation-state, who will determine what rights are distributed, when, and to whom? The United States is the favorite candidate to fill that role, preferred by the world's multiculturalist crowd, even though the United Nations puts dictatorships in charge of its own human rights committees and is itself as corrupt as the countries it seeks to influence. The U.N. can no more be trusted to guarantee American freedom than the former Soviet Union could have, nor should it be required to do so. A worldwide plebiscite or global economy with six billion voters is not the answer. In truth, I would fear the results such votes would bring.

Citizenship should be as important to Americans as it was to the ancient Romans. In every sense, citizenship is a set of rights (voting, equal protection under the law, etc.) and responsibilities (draft registry, jury duty, etc.). But at its core, citizenship is about belonging. It is an allegiance you owe to your nation and an allegiance your nation owes to you. Citizenship is more than residency; it is more than an address; it's more than an electric bill. It's part of who we are and a source of pride. Much more than the value of citizenship is lost when we abandon our national heritage. And when you take away a belief that it is something special to be an American, something else can—and likely will—fill the void.

I believe the greatest attack on the fabric holding America together has been the purposeful avoidance of the enforcement of our laws pertaining to citizenship and immigration. When you couple that with the fact that America no longer requires immigrants to assimilate into our culture, we have a recipe for disaster.

It is telling that although solid majorities of average Americans, in numerous polls and surveys, indicate they overwhelmingly support assimilation and citizenship requirements, "official" America—those in academia, the media, the courts, and many in government—don't agree, despite the plethora of laws requiring such compliance. Immigrants, therefore, aren't induced to learn our language; they aren't expected to learn our history; we don't insist they adopt our customs, observe our holidays, or respect our traditional religious underpinnings. In essence, we don't expect them to become Americans—just "residents."

It's no wonder that the United States is becoming polarized and balkanized. We have set ourselves up to dissolve into a nation dissimilar, disparate, and fragmented. Who doubts that someday we will wake up and find we are no longer one nation but a conglomeration of several small nations that lack commonality? We know what happened in the Balkans—Serbs, Croatians, and Bosnian Muslims went to war with each other, though before the collapse of the Soviet Union, all were "united" under a communist banner.

It's not as if the problem has not been addressed.

Officially, the United States has a vast array of laws, policies, and regulations governing immigration and citizenship. It would be grossly unfair for me to say that none of the scores of public servants, law-enforcement personnel, and other officials responsible for immigration and citizenship are trying to make things better. But clearly the federal government as a whole is failing to do all it can.

If the root cause of our impending diversification disaster is our failure as a nation to require millions of new immigrants to assimilate into *our* culture, learn *our* history, and become part of *American* society, then the blame must rest with the advocacy of an unofficial open-borders policy. It is a policy pursued by a powerful coalition of lawmakers, corporations, and advocacy groups who see our national borders as an impediment to progress, an anachronism in these "enlightened" times of global communications, commerce, and travel—even though our country achieved its historic superpower status without cause or need to sacrifice the integrity of our borders. Indeed, victory in World War II—which defined our status as the world's most powerful nation—was fought on the premise of preserving our national existence. In a very real sense, the war against the practitioners of terrorism we fight today is also a fight to the death.

Americans formerly understood the value of citizenship and the dangers of unchecked immigration without assimilation. As President Theodore Roosevelt observed in a 1907 speech:

> In the first place we should insist that if the immigrant who comes here in good faith becomes an American and assimilates himself to us, he shall be treated on an exact equality with everyone else, for it is an outrage to discriminate against any such man because of creed, or birthplace, or origin. But this is predicated upon the man's becoming in very fact an American, and nothing but an American. . . . There can be no divided allegiance here. Any man who says he is an American, but something else also, isn't an American at all. We have room for but one flag, the American flag, and this excludes the red

flag, which symbolizes all wars against liberty and civilization, just as much as it excludes any foreign flag of a nation to which we are hostile. . . . We have room for but one language here, and that is the English language . . . and we have room for but one sole loyalty and that is a loyalty to the American people.[5]

In a separate speech before the Knights of Columbus in 1912, he added:

There is no room in this country for hyphenated Americanism. When I refer to hyphenated Americans, I do not refer to naturalized Americans. Some of the very best Americans I have ever known were naturalized Americans, Americans born abroad. But a hyphenated American is not an American at all. This is just as true of the man who puts "native" before the hyphen as of the man who puts German or Irish or English or French before the hyphen. Americanism is a matter of the spirit and of the soul. Our allegiance must be purely to the United States. We must unsparingly condemn any man who holds any other allegiance.[6]

In more modern times, President Ronald Reagan sounded the alarm about our citizenship and immigration crisis. "The simple truth is that we've lost control of our own borders, and no nation can do that and survive," he said.[7]

Multiculturalists will try to convince us that it is arrogant, racist, and bigoted to insist that immigrants entering our country should adopt our culture. But they're wrong. It is not bigoted to bring this problematic issue to light and to insist we have a national dialogue about it. In fact, it's a courageous thing to do. There are now between twelve million and twenty million illegal aliens in the United States, with more coming every month. How many more can America take in, especially if they aren't coming to be citizens?

Attempts to fix the problem in the past have been weak and ineffective. For example, the amnesty for illegal immigrants incorporated in the 1986 Immigration Reform and Control Act actually increased illegal immigration dramatically, as family members came to America to join their three million legalized relatives. Instead of solving the illegal immigration problem, amnesty triggered an increase of half a million illegals crossing the border per year. Today immigration reform bills do nothing more than repeat the same mistakes of the past.

Why so many migrants are coming here and staying is easy to explain. In Mexico and the Latin American countries from which most migrants come—legal or otherwise—there are few opportunities to make a better life. In the United States, by comparison, such opportunities abound. Employers are supposed to be fined severely for hiring illegal workers under the 1986 reforms. As it turns out, immigration officials barely enforce these sanctions: fines issued to employers dropped more than 90 percent from 1992 to 2003, investigations of employers dropped more than 70 percent during the late 1990s, and arrests were almost nonexistent. Illegal immigrants were attracted to jobs offered by unscrupulous employers who didn't fear punishment.

The 1986 amnesty and the subsequent tidal wave of immigrants also exerted downward pressure on the wages of low-skilled workers in the United States—legal and illegal. Not surprisingly, business interests took advantage of the cheap labor and have become, over the decades, addicted to it. They have pushed Congress and the president to propose reckless guest-worker programs.

These are not racist statements, they are truths. And until more Americans use these truths and face down the raging multiculturalists who yell, "Racist!" because they can't argue with these truths, nothing will change.

NOT THERE YET

THERE ARE times when the people's elected representatives appear to understand what's going on. For example, President George W. Bush—himself a former governor of Texas, the state with the longest border with Mexico—said in a speech to an audience in Grapevine, Texas, in August 2005: "We've got to do something about our immigration laws. Our obligation is to secure the borders. We've got to make sure that we have the resources and technologies available for our Border Patrol agents. We've got to make sure we have a focused strategy to prevent people, goods, drugs, whatever, from being smuggled into this country. That's one of our duties."[8]

Others have also spoken out. New Mexico Governor Bill Richardson, a Democrat and former energy secretary under President Bill Clinton, in justifying his decision to declare a state of emergency along his state's border with Mexico in August 2005, said: "I have a responsibility to protect our citizens, property and communities. The southern border . . . has been devastated by the ravages of terror and human smuggling, drug smuggling, kidnapping, murder, destruction and the death of livestock. . . . [It] is in an extreme state of disrepair and is inadequately funded or safeguarded to protect the lives and property of . . . citizens."[9]

Within days of Richardson's announcement, Governor Janet Napolitano of Arizona, also a Democrat, followed suit and declared a state of emergency along her state's common border with Mexico.

I called on Governors Arnold Schwarzenegger and Rick Perry—Republican heads of state for California and Texas, respectively—to follow the lead of their Democratic colleagues so that each of the four southwestern border states would simultaneously be in a state of declared emergency over the dangers and destruction presented by the unofficial federal open-borders policy. I was hoping such unified action would spur Washington to action. Schwarzenegger balked, but Perry, in mid-October 2005, announced "a comprehensive blueprint for border security, which includes the use of the Texas National Guard for training and for deployment in emergencies."[10]

And in December 2005 I was able to spearhead an effort in the House to pass a major immigration reform bill—the most substantial of its kind in more than a decade. Formally known as the Border Protection, Antiterrorism, and Illegal Immigration Control Act of 2005, it would fund the construction of nearly seven hundred miles of a new, high-tech, double-tiered fence along the most heavily traveled areas of the southwestern border; it requires employers to verify the citizenship or legal residency status of all employees; it gives more authority to local law-enforcement authorities to arrest and detain illegal aliens; and it punishes so-called sanctuary cities (like Denver) that protect and aid illegal migrants by forbidding local authorities from apprehending them or even helping federal officials to apprehend them.

It was a substantial reform bill with real provisions and real changes I have fought to enact during most of my years in public office. I applauded the bill's provisions as cogent, rational, appropriate, and responsible. For seven years prior to its passage I had been talking to anyone in the Congress who would listen about our nation's border crisis, so I was happy to see such progress.

But this progress was short-lived.

Many backers of the initiatives turned out to be fair-weather supporters, offering more words than action. Their subsequent inaction speaks the loudest, and this has generally been the case when the issue turns to immigration and citizenship. The problem is that strong words without strong action will not keep America safe from outside threats. And it won't keep America safe from the internal threats building from so much immigration.

Many congressmen back President Bush's "solution" to the problem, which is the implementation of a so-called guest-worker program, a plan that amounts to little more than an altered form of amnesty (as we discussed in previous chapters). But given our porous borders, any discussion of his plan is purely theoretical. After all, why would prospective immigrants submit to a government plan that constrains their travel, their work options, and their stay in the United States when they can so easily come here illegally?

As to the state governors, they have done little as well. In the case of Governor Richardson of New Mexico, his state was given one million dollars in emergency grant funds to help pay for extra border-enforcement personnel and tools. But a story I read in the *Las Cruces Sun News* on September 27, 2005, said that at least one of the border sheriffs was using his grant money to monitor the Minutemen—the civilian volunteers who set up operations along portions of the U.S. border that are often breached by illegal immigrants—and "enforce county ordinances and state statutes."

In a letter to Governor Richardson, I asked him to "direct state funding in your command to combating illegal immigration, not obstructing volunteers who want to help." And I added, "Given your new rhetoric on border security and your emergency declaration, I had hoped that you might actually change the way you govern your state.

But, after the cameras left and the satellite trucks drove away, it appears to be business as usual for your administration." He denied any part of those emergency funds were going for things other than border enforcement, but I couldn't accept that.

After accusing me of doing nothing but "blustering" about illegal immigration, I wrote him again and challenged him to debate the issue with me in public: "I ask you to present your views about immigration and border security in a debate with me, as our schedules permit." I'm still waiting for his office to contact me.[11]

The episodes with the state governors and the lack of progress following the approval of my favorite immigration-reform measures makes the point well that one reason why immigration and citizenship issues don't get traction is because they are too often politicized for selfish reasons by judges, politicians, educators, and bureaucrats.

MALIGNANT MULTICULTURALISM

THE RADICAL cult of multiculturalism also undermines the issue of immigration and assimilation. As a movement, it is a malignancy that essentially opposes the idea of a common culture, and actually serves to reject assimilation and commonality as necessary components to a successful, enduring society. Once the ideology of multiculturalism turns cultlike and malevolent, it transforms itself into a sort of ethnocentrism—a belief among members of one ethnic group that they are superior to all others.

The problem is, this malignancy is already in the advanced stages. For instance, in September 2005, a senior at Larkin High School in Elgin, Illinois—a suburb of Chicago—was reprimanded and sent to the principal's office because he remained seated during the playing of the Mexican national anthem at a ceremony, during school hours, honoring Mexican independence day. The seventeen-year-old was in the process of enlisting in the U.S. military and was afraid honoring another country's anthem might somehow jeopardize his status.[12]

"I am concerned that the Mexican-Americans have unfairly monopolized the teaching of cultural awareness at this school," the boy's father told the local newspaper. "At least that's the perspective of a parent. I'd love to be corrected."[13]

School officials, however, defended the celebration. School board president Ken Kaczynski said, "If we were teaching one culture's history over another, then we have an issue. But I don't think that's the case." And yet, it *was* the case.

This student was no stranger to such "controversy." In the spring of 2005 he wrote an essay lamenting the celebration of *Mexican* holidays in *American* schools. He faulted Mexican students, saying they should not have lowered the American flag in favor of the Mexican flag months earlier on September 16, 2004, again in celebration of Mexican independence day. Of the approximately 2,250 students at that high school, 38.8 percent are Hispanic and nearly one-quarter are brand-new to English. Still, said the boy's father, "If they have an assembly, I would be happy if they will not try to force students to honor patriotic elements of another culture unless they also honor our flag, our anthem as well."[14]

Incidents such as this are not confined to the Chicago area. The Roy Rogers–Dale Evans Museum, an old-West cavalry-style fort that was, for decades, situated along Highway 15 in the high Mojave Desert in California, packed up and moved to Branson, Missouri, in the spring of 2003. The reason? A transformation in the cultural nature of the region so reduced interest and attendance, it became irrelevant. New, mostly Hispanic, immigrants settling in California are not absorbing the cultural history of the region or of the country. In a *New York Times* interview, Rosalina Sondoval-Marin, who was having a beer in the El Chubasco bar on historic Route 66, scoffed, "Roy Rogers? He doesn't mean anything. There's a revolution going on, and it don't include no Roy Rogers or Bob Hope."[15]

Without question, the rot of multiculturalism has spread well beyond the public schools and college campuses into our daily lives. And because of that, the vast majority of Americans who are not subscribers to the ideology are nonetheless forced to deal with its raging intolerance of traditional America:

- After a Young America's Foundation Event at Ithaca College featuring Bay Buchanan, homosexual and feminist student activists demanded that the event be declared "biased" by the school's Bias-related Incident Committee. Although the speech was not ruled biased, committee hearings to determine whether an "incident" occurred were held behind closed doors. The accused was not to be informed of the committee's decision unless it determined that the student or student group should be referred to the judiciary committee. Meanwhile, discussions on changing the definition of "biased" were also held in private.

- Vanderbilt University renamed its Confederate Memorial Hall dormitory to Memorial Hall because the word "Confederate" made some people uncomfortable. Also, Vanderbilt assistant professor of mathematics Jonathan David Farley wrote in the *Nashville Tennessean* newspaper that Confederates were "cowards masquerading as civilized men" and that "every Confederate soldier deserved not a hallowed resting place at the end of his days but a reservation at the end of the gallows."[16] On his Web page, Farley placed a picture of himself posing next to a poster of Marxist Ernesto "Che" Guevara, whom Farley says he considers a hero.[17]

- Incoming freshmen at the University of North Carolina–Chapel Hill have been required to read *Approaching the Qur'an: The Early Revelations*. According to UNC chancellor James Moeser, the book was "chosen in the wake of September 11th," which was a "great opportunity to have a conversation on the teachings of one of the world's great religions." No word on whether incoming freshmen will have to read an introduction to the Bible, also representative of another of the world's "great religions."

- Texas school board administrators toned down the curriculum that teaches Texas independence by suppressing "us vs. them" perspectives in lessons about the Alamo and the state's independence from Mexico. According to the social studies curriculum manager of the Houston Independent School District, the school board administrators made the change because they don't want "Hispanic kids, or any kids, to feel like we're teaching a biased approach" to the history of Texas.

In his book, *50% American: Immigration and National Identity in an Age of Terrorism*, Stanley A. Renshon writes: "In the past four decades, because of substantial increases in immigration, America has become more racially, ethnically, and culturally diverse. At the same time, the country's cultural, social, and political institutions have been subjected to enormous pressure—domestically from multiculturalism and internationally from the rise of international cosmopolitanism. The latter urges that Americans turn away from their narrow national identifications in favor of transnational and international attachments."[18]

Should it even matter that America is "more racially, ethnically, and culturally diverse" now than at any other time in our history? I say it does matter. Today's immigrants have a much different attitude than immigrants who settled here one hundred years ago. This newer, postmodern wave of immigrants isn't assimilating into our culture because, unlike their predecessors, they have adopted a kind of parasitic approach to the United States. They aren't interested in becoming citizens; they simply want to *attach* themselves to their American host and feed off of it while maintaining their native identities and cultures. In doing so, they lack any sense of American community, which means they aren't interested in contributing to society, either.

Notes Renshon: "A community requires more than incidental membership and a what's-in-it-for-me calculus to function and prosper. Emotional attachments provide a community with the psychological resources to weather disappointments and disagreements, and help to maintain a community's resolve in the face of historic dangers."[19] It's hard to argue with that conclusion.

BECOME AMERICANS

THE ISSUE of immigration and citizenship matters because it carries with it important national security implications—a growing concern in today's world of terrorism. When our borders are unprotected and porous, people will cross them at will. It's just as simple as that. Admittedly, many come just to work, but an increasing number of others are using mass migration as a cover to get into our country to sell drugs, run weapons, and, we believe, plan terror attacks.

Cavalier attitudes about our borders should give us all national security nightmares. It's plain to me that there is an absolute and total connection between immigration, open borders, and our national security. It isn't just that one result of keeping those borders open is that people will come across with bombs or some sort of chemical or biological agent. Out-of-control immigration is also a threat to our national security because when it combines with the cult of multiculturalism, it becomes a dagger pointed right at the heart of America. So we have to understand it. We have to talk about it. We cannot be afraid to address it. How can we adequately protect ourselves from Islamic extremists and other terrorists if we cannot control the flow of commerce and travel across our own borders?

Most Americans are very aware of the threat. Nearly three out of four believe there will be another major terrorist attack in the United States sometime in the next five years. Some 41 percent of Americans believe an attack will come sooner, within two years. Another 14 percent believe another attack will happen within a year. As to the type of attack, roughly half of Americans believe it will involve a nuclear weapon or other weapon of mass destruction.[20]

In this mad rush to become the world's first earthbound utopia, we are, quite literally, diversifying ourselves to death. This realization is why I have spent so much time not only talking about the issues of immigration and citizenship but also trying (in Congress) to reform a system that is badly underutilized and overburdened. And while there are many problems associated with the general issues of "immigration and citizenship"—including loss of American jobs, the displacement of American workers, the negative effect on our economy—the most important of all of these is the loss of our American identity.

Oddly enough, while we seem disinterested in requiring immigrants to assimilate, we are going out of our way to require our own citizens to undergo "cultural diversity training" so we can better "understand" immigrant cultures. Instead of requiring immigrants to assimilate into our culture, we have required our own citizens to assimilate foreign cultures at the expense of our own. What kind of sense does that make?

I'm not asking immigrants to leave their ethnicity at our borders. What I am saying is we, as Americans, have to demand immigrants do what they supposedly came here to do: become Americans! As far as I'm concerned, this isn't about ethnicity. It's about numbers, costs, and most important, social and cultural cohesion.

As the saying goes, since the founding of America we have been a "land of immigrants." That's true as far as it goes, but today—more than two centuries removed from our birth as a nation—it can truthfully be said that we have developed a uniquely *American* culture and that we have given birth to many generations of *American* citizens.

It can also be said that, once upon a time, we expected our immigrants to speak our language (English, please!), worship in our (non-theocratic) churches, adopt our way of life, and pledge allegiance to our country. We can recapture this very successful formula, but it will require some work from all of us.

The very first thing we must do is recognize our uniquely American culture—language, religious freedom, values, beliefs—and promote them above all others.

We have to discard the self-destructive philosophy of radical multiculturalism that contributes to and exacerbates the problem of the balkanization of America.

We need to confer citizenship *only* on those who are desirous of severing all ties to their country of origin, who exhibit a genuine commitment to becoming an American in every sense of the word. And to limit or forbid residency to those who will not accept citizenship.

We must remind the world (and sadly, a growing number of our own people) that coming to and living in the United States is not a right. Staying here carries with it a duty to embrace and support the fundamental values that bind us together. As it stands, there are too many things pulling us apart and not enough bringing us together. But we need unity to preserve and protect a way of life more than 230 years in the making.

To be successful, we have to shun the language and thinking of the true anti-American racists and bigots who pose as patriots: the multiculturalists.

Unfortunately, there are still folks on the anti-American fringe of this issue who, because of their First Amendment right of free speech, cannot be stopped from spewing their venom and hate. For that reason, I want to appeal to all those who have labored so hard in this vineyard and who have done so out of a sincere concern for our country's future to join me in denouncing those who have only disgust in their hearts and a perverted view of race in their minds.

I believe that immigration and citizenship reform is so important that how we resolve this challenge will not only determine what kind of country we will be, but whether or not America will remain a country at all.

I am proud of what America is. I am proud of all it has accomplished or helped others to accomplish. I am proud of being a product of Western civilization. I am proud of the infrastructure. I am proud of the principles that we embody in the organization we call the Congress of the United States. I am proud that we have an adherence to the rule of the law. I am proud that we believe in and strongly defend the right to pursue our own religion and to speak openly about our feelings about government. All of these things are worthy of our allegiance and worthy things about which we should tell our children. We must encourage them with all our hearts. If we do not, we will find ourselves in mortal danger.

CONCLUSION

Your Assignment

Now that we have made a bulletproof case for the need to control immigration and for a critical look at multiculturalism, you didn't think that a former teacher would let you get off without an assignment, did you?

I have two assignments: yours and mine. Mine is to exert every effort to force our government to get a handle on immigration, both legal and illegal. Previously, I have laid out both long- and short-term strategies for reforming the government's control of this paramount issue. These strategies must be implemented from the top—at the Congress.

Someone must lead the Washington effort. In the absence of any other visible leadership, I have volunteered and will do my best. You can help this effort by telling your representatives and senators what you want them to do. Do that NOW!

Your specific assignment is to think harder about this question of an American culture. Is there such a thing? Is it different now for your generation than it was for your American ancestors? How? Why?

I submit that American culture did not change by itself over the last century. It was changed through a conscious effort by leftist elites to "reform" a school system that had been built on the classics and was based on a core curriculum of rich subject matter. This system produced an educated and English-speaking American people who shared common views of American origins, opinions, tastes, and thousands of ideas adding up to what has been described as an American "cultural literacy."

Most of the folks in the greatest generation were educated this way. Some have said that their high-school diplomas were more valuable than today's college degrees. But they were the end of an era. American schools began to change perceptibly in the 1950s with the abandonment of the traditional core curriculum.

Your assignment is to learn more about this so that you will have a better idea of what actually happened to the wonderful schools of your grandparents and so that you will see what must be done to recapture what we have lost: an American cultural literacy.

Your reading assignment consists of two specific books by E. D. Hirsch Jr.: *Cultural Literacy: What Every American Needs to Know* and *The Schools We Need, and Why We Don't Have Them.*

The earlier book was a bombshell in 1987 because it dared to suggest that there were five thousand things that every culturally literate American should know. It became the foundation for the Core Knowledge Curriculum, a magically successful course of study for kindergarten through eighth grade. Children are being blessed with this curriculum—and by the dedicated teachers who are using it—in hundreds of schools across the nation, many of them charter schools with long waiting lists for admission.

The second book is a review of our pathetic government school situation and some dynamite ideas on how to reverse their downward slide now endangering our culture.

Look, when you complain about the failure of immigrants to become assimilated into our culture, exactly what is it that you want them to blend with? Do you really care if they eat tamales or dance the tango or prefer truffles on Wheaties? I don't. I've already said we don't expect new Americans to check the positive things about their former cultures at the border. Many of those imports have been incorporated gracefully into our daily lives without problems.

But while they are bringing those old fashions with them, we expect them to crave a new citizenship here—gladly flinging off the loyalties to a *patria,* or native land, and donning the responsibilities of freedom. How would they know about or understand those new duties? Will they copy the young Americans they meet, 75 percent of whom can't even correctly describe the North American continent, to say nothing of speaking a foreign language.

The purpose of this assignment, then, is not just to help your understanding of our situation but also to equip you with a remedy for your own community. There may be other ways to correctly describe 'his American culture, but there is no other way I know of that is specifically designed to support the desperately needed reform of what is (or is not) being taught in our government schools.

Is this clear? Immigration reform stands on its own as a critical public issue. The status quo will condemn us to eventual takeover by cultures that are not just un-American but are literally deadly in their applications—the Muslim treatment of women as chattels, for instance. So the first defense of American culture is to reform immigration.

But we must look past the first defense to see if the current American culture is what we really want to be. Is it really worth saving? That's a question for the people to answer. And do we have the patience to wait for another generation of school kids to get it? That's how long it will take for the ship to right itself.

In the meantime, when our immigration-control efforts bear fruit, we will need a reliable, culturally literate, well educated—yes, and correctly motivated—very large pool of American job seekers eager for employment in a market not flooded with underpaid foreigners laboring under a serf mentality.

No lollygagging! Accept your assignment. Get the books. Take the quiz. Harass your school board. Work to be proud of a culturally literate, safe America!

NOTES

PREFACE

1. Jerry Seper, "Who's Behind These 'Marches'?" *Washington Times*, April 11, 2006.

CHAPTER 1: WHAT IT MEANT TO BE AN AMERICAN

1. Peggy Noonan, "The American Way: What Does It Mean That Your First Act on Entering a Country Is Breaking Its Laws?" *Wall Street Journal*, December 8, 2005.

CHAPTER 2: DESTROYING OUR ROOTS

1. Valerie Richardson, "Denver's Columbus Parade Turns into Free-Speech Issue," *Washington Times*, October 6, 2005.
2. Ibid.
3. Katlyn Carter, "Berkeley Celebrates Indigenous People's Day; Annual City Holiday Replaces Columbus Day," *Daily Californian*, October 10, 2005.
4. Ibid.
5. "Bar's Sign 'Affront' to Hispanics," Associated Press, October 9, 2005.
6. Ron Isaac, "Tongue-Tied," *EducationNews.org*, February 9, 2005.
7. *Lou Dobbs*, CNN transcript, August 25, 2005, http://transcripts.cnn.com/TRANSCRIPTS/0508/25/ldt.01.html.
8. Arthur M. Schlessinger Jr., "The Disunited of America," *American Educator* (Winter 1991).
9. Tom Tancredo, "Our Porous Borders," floor speech, House of Representatives, April 2, 2004.
10. David Kupelian, *The Marketing of Evil* (Nashville: WND Books, 2005), 103.

CHAPTER 3: IMPARTING THE CULT OF MULTICULTURALISM

1. Ward Churchill, "Some People Push Back: On the Justice of Roosting Chickens," *Dark Night Field Notes*, September 12, 2001.
2. Robert Jensen, "U.S. Just as Guilty of Committing Own Violent Acts," *Houston Chronicle*, September 26, 2001.
3. "Jihad on Campus," *New York Sun*, December 14, 2005.
4. Jim Nelson Black, "A Crisis on Campus," *Whistleblower*, September 2005.

5. Scott Norvell, "Successfully Stopping Santa and A-Caroling We Won't Go," Fox News, December 15, 2003.

6. Suzanne Fields, "The Jihad Against Textbooks," *Washington Times,* February 20, 2003.

7. See Thomas Babington Macaulay, *Lays of Ancient Rome: With Fury and the Armada* (1842; repr., Washington DC: Regnery, 1997).

8. Will Durant, *The Story of Civilization,* vol. 3, *Caesar and Christ* (New York: Simon and Schuster, 1944), 366, quoted by David Keene, "Dual Allegiance and the Politics of Immigration Reform" (panel discussion transcript, Hudson Institute Center for American Common Culture and the Center for Immigration Studies, November 30, 2005), http://www.cis.org/articles/2005/back1205 transcript.html.

CHAPTER 5: CLASH OF THE CIVILIZATIONS

1. Winston Churchill, *The River War* (London: Longmans, Green & Co., 1899), 11:248–50.

2. Paul L. Williams, *The Dunces of Doomsday* (Nashville: WND Books, 2006), 55–58.

3. Ann Coulter, "Future Widows of America: Write Your Congressman," September 27, 2001, http://www.townhall.com/opinion/columns/anncoulter/2001/09/27/167762.html.

4. Steven Stalinsky, "Kingdom Comes to North America," *National Review Online,* May 13, 2004, http://www.nationalreview.com/comment/stalinsky200405130846.asp.

5. Magdi Abdelhadi, "Controversial Preacher with 'Star Status,'" BBC News, July 7, 2004, http://news.bbc.co.uk/2/hi/uk_news/3874893.stm.

6. "Hezbollah: Death to America," *Newsmax.com,* April 18, 2003, http://www.newsmax.com/archives/articles/2003/4/17/195849.shtml.

7. James G. Week, "Al Qaeda: Worse Coming," *New York Daily News,* September 8, 2003, http://www.nydailynews.com/front/story/115832p-104402c.html.

8. "Al Qaeda Threatens More UK, U.S. Attacks," *CNN.com,* August 4, 2005, http://www.cnn.com/2005/WORLD/meast/08/04/zawahiri.london/.

9. "Transcript of Bin Laden tape," Associated Press, January 19, 2006, http://www.usatoday.com/news/world/2006-01-19-binladen-fulltext-x.html.

10. Samuel P. Huntington, "The Clash of Civilizations," *Foreign Affairs* 72 no. 3 (Summer 1993), http://www.alamut.com/subj/economics/misc/clash.html.

11. Paula Reed Ward, "Memorial's Crescent Shape Criticized as Inappropriate," *Pittsburgh Post-Gazette,* September 10, 2005.

12. A. M. Siriano, "Is It Time Yet for a Crusade?" *Men's News Daily,* September 13, 2005.

13. Michelle Malkin, "Monumental Surrender," Creators Syndicate, September 14, 2005.

14. Sher Zieve, "9/11 Memorial Hijacking: CAIR Again Plays Race Card," *Men's News Daily,* September 15, 2005.

15. Dimitri Vassilaros, "Kill the Crescent," *Pittsburgh Tribune-Review,* September 16, 2005.

16. Paula Reed Ward, "Designer of Flight 93 Memorial Receptive to Changes," *Pittsburgh Post-Gazette,* September 16, 2005.

CHAPTER 6: THE BARBARIANS ARE PAST THE GATE

1. Jon E. Dougherty, "Al-Qaeda Evidence Along U.S. Border?" *WorldNetDaily .com,* November 26, 2005.

2. Malini Bawa, "Counter-terrorists Worry About Illegal Immigration," *VOA News,* November 30, 2005, http://www.voanews.com/english/archive/2005–11 /2005–11–30-voa35.cfm?CFID=24799171&CFTOKEN=30537480.

3. "U.S. Border Patrol Facing New Illegal Immigration Problems," *Voices,* June 30, 2005, http://www.voicesmag.com/Archives/News/june2005 /us_border_patrol_new_problem_063005.

4. Jon E. Dougherty, "Lawmaker: Terror War Spilling Across Border," *WorldNetDaily.com,* November 16, 2005.

5. Wikipedia, http://en.wikipedia.org/wiki/Mara_Salvatrucha.

6. "Border Sheriff Warns: We're Overwhelmed," *WorldNetDaily.com,* November 12, 2005.

7. Mike Sunnucks, "Arrest Adds to Fears of Terrorist Presence on Mexican Border," *Business Journal,* November 22, 2005, http://phoenix.bizjournals.com /phoenix/stories/2005/11/21/daily23.html.

CHAPTER 7: AUTUMN IN BESLAN

1. Bill Gertz, "Chechen Terrorists Probed," *Washington Times,* October 13, 2005.

2. Paul Marshall, "Four Million," *National Review Online,* August 27, 2004.

CHAPTER 8: OUR POROUS BORDERS

1. U.S. Census Bureau figures, January 2006.

2. Federation of American Immigration Reform estimate based on U.S. Census Bureau figures, January 2006.

3. Cited in "Our Porous Borders," 108th Cong., 2nd sess., *Congressional Record* 150 (April 2, 2004): H2144, http://thomas.loc.gov/cgi-bin/query/F?r 108:1:./temp/~r108x1jTs8:e0.

4. Ibid.

5. Diana Hull, "World Affairs Report: Houston, Texas," http://wais.stanford.edu/USA/us_houston1.html (accessed November 13, 2005).

6. Stephan Dinan and Jerry Seper, "House Approves Border Fence," *Washington Times,* December 16, 2005.

7. Abbie Stillie, "On the Border," *Fairbanks (AK) Daily News-Miner,* April 20, 2005.

CHAPTER 9: THE MYTHS OF IMMIGRATION

1. "Tom Tancredo's Wall," *Wall Street Journal,* December 29, 2005.

CHAPTER 10: SYSTEM BREAKDOWN

1. Michelle Malkin, "Open Doors for Hezbollah," *National Review,* November 14, 2005.

2. Stephen Dinan, "Mexican ID Not Valid, A 'Threat,' FBI Says," *Washington Times,* December 6, 2005.

3. Ibid.

4. Will Dunham, "Rumsfeld Says U.S. Constrained in Information War," Reuters, February 1, 2006.

CHAPTER 11: POLITICS OF IMMIGRATION

1. "President Discusses Border Security and Immigration Reform in Arizona," White House News & Policies, November 28, 2005, http://www.whitehouse.gov/news/releases/2005/11/20051128–7.html.

2. James R. Edwards Jr., "Congressional Consensus Slow on Immigration," *Human Events,* September 19, 2005, http://www.humaneventsonline.com/article.php?id=9144.

3. United States Conference of Catholic Bishops, Office of Migration and Refugee Policy Web site, http://www.usccb.org/mrs/mrp.shtml (accessed February 18, 2006).

4. "Justice for Immigrants" Parish Kit, *Ideas for Schools: Youth,* 2.

5. Ibid., pt. 2: *Suggested Parish Committees and Tasks,* 3.

6. Sara A. Carter, "Border Watchers Want DC's Attention," *Inland Valley Daily Bulletin,* February 5, 2006.

7. Ibid.

8. Ibid.

9. Ibid.

10. Ibid.

CHAPTER 12: BREACH IN SECURITY

1. Michelle Malkin, "A Heartless Homeland Security Screw-up,"

Townhall.com, January 26, 2005, http://townhall.com/opinion/columns /michellemalkin/2005/01/26/14347.html.

2. "About Y-12," Y-12 National Security Complex Web Site, http://www.y12 .doe.gov/about/.

3. Ibid.

4. Terence P. Jeffrey, "Oak Ridge: Our De Facto Border," *Human Events,* June 27, 2005.

5. "Nuclear Plant Cheated in Terrorist Drill," Associated Press, January 27, 2004, http://www.newsmax.com/archives/articles/2004/1/26/141320.shtml.

6. Justine Redman, "Congressional Investigators Find Flaws in Port Security," *CNN.com,* May 26, 2005, http://www.cnn.com/2005/POLITICS/05/26 /port.security/index.html.

7. Ibid.

8. "Port Security: Shipping Containers," The Subcommittee on Coast Guard and Maritime Transportation, March 13, 2002, http://www.house.gov /transportation/cgmt/03–13–02/03–13–02memo.html.

9. "Arab Purchase of Port Firms Raises Fears in U.S.," *Baltimore Sun,* February 16, 2006.

10. Ibid.

11. "Arab Takeover of U.S. Ports Seen as Security 'Insanity,'" *WorldNetDaily .com,* February 15, 2006, http://www.wnd.com/news/article.asp?ARTICLE _ID=48845.

12. Michelle Malkin, "Who's Watching the White House?" Townhall.com, January 3, 2003.

13. "NYPD: Explosives Vanish from Airport," *WorldNetDaily.com,* November 23, 2003, http://wnd.com/news/article.asp?ARTICLE_ID=35776.

14. "Security Breach Shuts Down Los Alamos Lab," Associated Press, July 18, 2004, http://www.koat.com/news/3544240/detail.html.

15. Michelle Malkin, "Homeland Insecurity: The Year in Review," Townhall .com, December 29, 2004.

16. Jerry Seper, "Border Agents Put on Happy Face," *Washington Times,* August 27, 2004.

17. "D.C. Security Data Given to Terror-Tied Protest Group," WorldNetDaily .com, January 19, 2005, http://wnd.com/news/article.asp?ARTICLE_ID =42454.

18. Barbara Starr, "Navy Investigates Carrier Security Breach," CNN, May 10, 2005.

CHAPTER 13: MEXICO'S LAWLESS BORDER

1. Ray Suarez, "A Conversation with Vicente Fox," *NewsHour with Jim*

Lehrer, March 21, 2000, http://www.pbs.org/newshour/bb/latin_america/jan-june00/fox_3–21.html.

2. "President Bush, Mexican President Fox Reaffirm Commitment to Security," White House News and Policies, March 2004, http://www.whitehouse.gov/news/releases/2004/03/20040306-html.

3. Geri Smith, "Mapping the Way to a Border Flap," *Business Week*, January 25, 2006.

4. "Border Map Handout Halted," Associated Press, January 27, 2006, http://www.dallasnews.com/sharedcontent/dws/news/world/stories/DN-mexmaps_27int.ART.State.Edition1.1daf92ab.html.

5. "Guide for the Mexican Migrant," as found on the Web site: http://www.amren.com/mexguide/mexguide.html.

6. Billy House, "Hayworth Blasts Mexico Border-Crossing Comic Book," *Arizona Republic*, January 6, 2005, http://www.azcentral.com/specials/special03/articles/0106hayworth-mexic006.html.

7. Jerry Seper, "Border Task Force Seizes Weapons Cache in Texas," *Washington Times*, February 4, 2006.

8. Chris Hawley, "U.S. Pays Mexico to Secure Border," *Arizona Republic*, December 29, 2005.

9. Ibid.

10. Ibid.

CHAPTER 14: THE ECONOMICS OF MASS MIGRATION

1. "The Estimated Cost of Illegal Immigration," Federation of American Immigration Reform policy paper, http://www.fairus.org/site/PageServer?pagename=iic_immigrationissuecentersf134 (accessed February 21, 2006).

2. "Breaking the Piggy Bank: How Illegal Immigration Is Sending Schools into the Red," *Federation for American Immigration Reform*, updated June 2005, http://www.fairus.org/site/PageServer?pagename=research_researchf6ad (accessed February 21, 2006).

3. Ibid.

4. Heather McDonald, "Crime and the Illegal Alien," *Center for Immigration Reform*, June 2004.

5. Ibid.

6. Jon E. Dougherty, "Illegal Immigration's Financial Impact," *Freedom Alliance Policy Paper*, http://www.freedomalliance.org/view_article.php?a_id=642.

7. Office of Management and Budget, Executive Office of the President, *The Budget of the United States Government, Fiscal Year 2006* (Washington DC: Government Printing Office, 2006).

8. Robert Samuelson, "Why U.S. Doesn't Need Guest Workers," *Newsweek,* March 22, 2006.

9. Steven Camarota, "The High Cost of Cheap Labor," *Center for Immigration Studies,* August 2004.

10. Ibid.

CHAPTER 15: THE THREAT TO OUR HEALTH SYSTEM BY ILLEGAL IMMIGRATION

1. Madeleine Pelner Cosman, "Illegal Aliens and American Medicine," *Journal of American Physicians and Surgeons* 10, no. 1 (Spring 2005).

2. Madeleine Pelner Cosman, "The Seen and Unseen," *Journal of American Physicians and Surgeons* 10, no. 1 (Spring 2005).

3. Cosman, "Illegal Aliens and American Medicine."

4. "Illegal Aliens Threaten U.S. Medical System," *WorldNetDaily.com,* March 13, 2005, http://www.worldnetdaily.com/news/article.asp?ARTICLE_ID=43275.

5. Cosman, "The Seen and Unseen."

6. Jon E. Dougherty, "Anchors Away," *Voices,* May 10, 2005.

7. Ibid.

8. "Illegal Aliens Threaten U.S. Medical System," *WorldNetDaily.com,* March 13, 2005.

9. Testimony of John C. Eastman before the House Judiciary Committee's Subcommittee on Immigration, Border Security and Claims, September 29, 2005, 2–4.

10. Ibid.

11. Cosman, "Illegal Aliens and American Medicine."

CHAPTER 16: ENVIRONMENTAL IMPACT FROM ILLEGAL IMMIGRATION

1. 2000 Current Population Survey, U.S. Census Bureau.

2. The Population-Environment Connection, FAIR (Federation for American Immigration Reform), http://www.fairus.org/site/PageServer?pagename=iic_immigrationissuecentersfd36.

3. Data derived from David Pimental and Marie Giampietro, "Food, Land, Population and the U.S. Economy," http://www.balance.org/articles/factsheet 2001.html.

4. For a thorough analysis of carrying capacity and the impact of population growth on the environment, see Californians for Population Stabilization at http://www.cap-s.org/main.html.

CHAPTER 18: PRESERVING OUR NATIONAL EXISTENCE

1. Debate in Denver, January 4, 2006.

2. Acts 22:26, KJV.

3. Acts 23:23–24, KJV.

4. "Life of Theodore Roosevelt," Theodore Roosevelt Association, http://www .theodoreroosevelt.org/life/Morocco.html.

5. John Fonte, "To 'Possess the National Consciousness of an American,'" *Center for Immigration Studies,* http://www.cis.org/articles/cantigny/fonte.html.

6. Theodore Roosevelt, "Hyphenated Americanism" speech to Knights of Columbus in New York City, October 12, 1915.

7. Ronald Reagan quoted in Jon E. Dougherty, *Illegals: The Imminent Threat Posed by Our Unsecured U.S.-Mexico Border* (Nashville: WND Books, 2004), 117.

8. President George W. Bush, speech in Grapevine, Texas, August 3, 2005.

9. Gov. Bill Richardson, speech in Columbus, New Mexico, August 12, 2005.

10. "Texas Governor Hot over Border Security," *WorldNetDaily.com,* October 13, 2005.

11. "Tancredo: Put Your Money Where Your Mouth Is, Guv," *The Hill,* October 6, 2005.

12. "Student Who Sat for Mexican Anthem Rebuked," *WorldNetDaily.com,* October 7, 2005.

13. Ibid.

14. Ibid.

15. Charlie LeDuff, "Roy Rogers and Dale Evans Ride Off to Missouri," *New York Times,* August 1, 2003.

16. Jonathan David Farley, "Remnants of the Confederacy Glorifying a Time of Tyranny," *Nashville Tennessean,* November 20, 2002.

17. Samuel Francis, "Some Genocides Are More Politically Correct than Others," *Creators Syndicate,* December 9, 2002.

18. Stanley A. Renshon, "Reforming Dual Citizenship in the United States," *Center for Immigration Studies,* October 2005.

19. Ibid.

20. Jon E. Dougherty, "Border Bureaucracy Worsens National Security," *Voices,* August 8, 2005.

INDEX

Abu Gheith, Suleiman, 97

Achenbrenner, Gale, 174

Adams, John, 46, 49

African Dress Day, 49

Agua Prieta, Mexico, 83

Aguirre, Eduardo, 119–20, 123

AIM (American Indian Movement), 25–26, 113

al Qaeda, 72, 79, 82, 84, 86, 97, 125

Alarcon, Erasmo, Jr., 85

Al-Najdi, Abu Abdel-Rahman, 72

Alneda (al Qaeda Web site), 97

Al-Qaradawi, Yusef, 70

al-Sadr, Muqtada, 82

al-Sudayyis, Abd al-Rahman, 70

al-Zawahiri, Ayman, 72

American Immigration Lawyers Association, 121

American Indian Movement (AIM), 25–26, 113

amnesty, 14, 128–33, 196–97, 199

anchor babies, 166–169, 171

Anderson, Max, 27

Arizona, 27–28, 83, 87, 101, 103, 114–15, 145, 157, 174, 177–78, 198

Ashton, Rick, 53–54, 56–58, 61, 63

Aurora, CO, 64, 102

Barlett, Donald L., 111, 173

Barnes, Gerald R., 131

Beamer, Todd, 74

bilingualism, 13, 34, 53, 55–59, 61, 63

Bill of Rights, 34, 44, 132

bin Laden, Osama, 70, 72, 77, 85, 93, 97

Black, Jim Nelson, 46

Black History Month, 49

Blunt, Roy, 187

Bonner, Robert, 142

Border Protection, Antiterrorism, and Illegal Immigration Control Act (H.R.4437), 131–32, 198

Boyles, Peter, 63

Bradley, Ed, 102

Brownsville, TX, 80

Bureau of Customs and Border Protection, 147

Burnett, Tom, Sr., 75

Bush, George H. W., 47

Bush, George W., 9, 11, 42, 65, 72, 93, 117, 128–29, 137, 144, 155, 197, 199

CAIR (Council on American-Islamic Relations), 73, 75

Californians for Population Stabilization (CAPS), 175

CAPS (Californians for Population Stabilization), 175

Chavez, Cesar, 49

cheap labor, 106, 127, 135, 158–61, 197

Chechnya, 89, 92–93, 95, 97

Chertoff, Michael, 141, 149

Christian Science Monitor, 191
Christianity and Christians, 41,
  66–68, 74, 77
Christmas, 39–40
Churchill, Ward, 43–45
Churchill, Winston, 66
City Club of Denver, 57
Civis Romanus, 192
Clark, Richard, 79
Clinton, Bill, 42, 77, 79, 128, 185–86,
  198
Columbine High School, 89, 91,
  93–94, 96
Columbus, Christopher, 25–27
Columbus Day, 25–27
Confederate Memorial Hall
  (Vanderbilt University), 202
Corona Research Group, 60
Coronado National Forest, 174
Cosman, Madeleine Pelner, 163, 165,
  171–72
Coulter, Ann, 68–69
Council on American-Islamic
  Relations (CAIR), 73
CRAG proposal, 171–72
Crockett, Davy, 47
C-SPAN, 135
Culberson, John, 86, 117

Declaration of Independence, 9, 33–34
Defense Intelligence Agency (DIA),
  49, 121–22
DeGenova, Nicholas, 44
DeLay, Tom, 11
Denver Post, 45
Denver Public Library (DPL), 13,
  53–64
Department of Defense, 76
Department of Energy, 138–39

Department of Homeland Security
  (DHS), 84, 86, 117, 120, 122–26,
  137, 140, 142, 146, 148–49, 158
Department of Immigration, 189
Department of Justice, 158
Derbez, Luis, 148
DHS (Department of Homeland
  Security), 84, 86, 117, 120,
  122–26, 137, 140, 142, 146,
  148–49, 158
DIA (Defense Intelligence Agency),
  49, 121–22
Divine, Robert, 121
Dobson, James, 41
Douglas, AZ, 39, 63, 177–78
DPL (Denver Public Library), 13,
  53–64
Dreier, David, 187
Dukakis, Michael, 47
Durant, Will, 52, 208

Eastman, John C., 169–70
Eichmann, Adolf, 43–44
El Paso, TX, 134
El Paso County, TX, 134
Ellis Island, 24
Emergency Medical Treatment and
  Active Labor Act (EMTALA)
  (S.1592), 164–65
EMTALA (Emergency Medical
  Treatment and Active Labor Act)
  (S.1592), 164–65
English-immersion, 28
European Union, 191

FAIR (Federation for American
  Immigration Reform), 156
Farabundo Matri National Liberation
  Front (FARC), 82, 142

FARC (Farabundo Matri National Liberation Front), 142
Farley, Jonathan David, 202
Fattah, Nadia Hussen, 169
FBI Joint Terrorism Task Force (JTTF), 86, 118. 122
FDNS (Fraud Detection and National Security), 121–22
Federation for American Immigration Reform (FAIR), 156
Fessio, Joseph, 68
Fields, Suzanne, 49
First Data Corporation, 11
Fort Worth Star-Telegram, 32
Fourteenth Amendment, 167, 170
Fox, Vicente, 143–46, 153
Fraud Detection and National Security (FDNS), 121–22
Friedman, Gregory H., 138–39

Gallagher, Dennis, 25, 28
globalization, 191
Golden, CO, 64
Gonzalez, Sigifredo, Jr., 84
Grand Mosque of Mecca, 70
Guantanamo Bay, Cuba, 170
guest-worker program, 119, 125, 128–30, 199
Gutierrez, Luiz, 127

H.R.2330/S.1033 (Secure America and Orderly Immigration Act), 132
H.R.3333 (Real Guest Act), 130
H.R.4437 (Border Protection, Antiterrorism, and Illegal Immigration Control Act), 131–32, 198
Hamdi, Esam Fouad, 169–70
Hamdi, Nadiah Hussen, 169–70
Hamdi, Yaser Esam, 169–70

Hart, Gary, 191
Hayworth, J. D., 87, 145
health-care system, 13, 160, 163–65, 171
Heatherly, Charles, 81
Hezbollah, 71–72, 80–81, 118
Hickenlooper, John W., 26, 53
Hirsch, E. D., Jr., 208
Hispanic Caucus, 30
Hispanic Human Resources Association, 30
Hooper, Ibrahim, 75
House Immigration Reform Caucus, 167, 187
House International Relations Committee, 95
House Judiciary Committee, 119, 169
Howard, Jacob, 167
Hudspeth County, TX, 133–34, 147–49
Hull, Diana, 175
Human Rights Commission, 144
Huntington, Samuel, 14, 65, 70, 72, 83
Hussein, Saddam, 186
Hutchinson, Asa, 142

IAC (International Action Center), 142
ICE (Immigration and Customs Enforcement), 117, 120, 150
illegal immigrants, 14, 21, 23, 53, 55, 80, 82, 89, 102–6, 108, 110, 111–15, 129, 131–34, 138–39, 141, 149, 155–61, 163–68, 171, 173–75, 177–78, 187–88, 196–99
illegal immigration, 12, 23, 83, 102–3, 107–15, 128, 130–32, 134, 143, 145–46, 155, 158–59, 161, 163,

165–67, 169, 171–75, 177, 179,
196–200
Immigration and Customs
Enforcement (ICE), 117, 120, 150
Immigration and Naturalization
Service (INS) (incorporated into the
Department of Homeland Security
in 2003), 117–18, 120, 123
Immigration Reform Caucus, 119,
167, 187
incursions, Mexican border (armed),
146–50, 153–54, 193
*Inland Valley (Ontario, CA) Daily
Bulletin,* 134
INS, *see above* Immigration and
Naturalization Service
International Action Center (IAC),
142
Iranian Diaspora, 73
Islamification, 74
Islamofascism, 15, 65–66, 77

Jefferson, Thomas, 21, 34, 46, 49
Jensen, Robert, 44
Jim Hogg County, TX, 85
Joint Terrorism Task Force (JTTF;
FBI), 86, 118, 122

Kaczynski, Ken, 201
Kennedy, John F., 29
Khobar Towers, 72
King, Peter, 114
Koran, the, 67–68, 77, 90
Kniazev, Eugueni, 137
Krikorian, Mark, 101
Kupelian, David, 35

La Raza, 15, 32
La Voz Nueva (Denver, CO), 56

Lakewood, CO, 64
Laredo, TX, 150
Las Cruces (NM) Sun News, 199
League of United Latin American
Citizens (LULAC), 15
Lincoln, Abraham, 46, 49
Livingstone, Ken, 70
Los Alamos National Laboratory, 141
Los Angeles County, CA, 83, 164
Los Zetas, 85
LULAC (League of United Latin
American Citizens), 15

Maastricht Treaty, 191
Macaulay, Thomas, 50–51
Machiavelli, Niccolò, 79
Madison, James, 49
Madrinas, 151–54
Mahbubani, Kishore, 65
Mainella, Fran, 75
Malkin, Michelle, 74, 137
Martinez-Gonzalez, Salvador, 141
Masling, Bob, 134
Matamoros, Mexico, 80
matricula consular card, 124, 188
May, Joe, 28
Mazar-e-Sharif, 169
Mill, John Stuart, 29
Milosevic, Slobodan, 186
Minutemen, 12, 134, 144, 199
Moeser, James, 202
Mohammed (the Prophet), 67–67, 77
Mojave Desert, 201
Morin, George, 173–74, 178
Morin, Linda, 173–74, 178
Mueller, Robert, Jr., 79–80
Muhammad, Khalid Sheikh, 97
multiculturalism, 9, 15, 22, 25, 27,
29, 34–35, 37–39, 41, 43, 45–47,

49, 50, 63, 73, 76–78, 183, 192, 200–201, 203–5, 207
Murdoch, Paul, 74, 76

NAFTA (North American Free Trade Agreement), 143
NAME (National Association for Multicultural Education), 45
Napolitano , Janet, 198
Nash, Gary B., 49
Nasrallah, Hassan, 71
National Association for Multicultural Education (NAME), 45
National Crime Information Center, 153
National Education Association (NEA), 42–43, 77
National Liberation Army, 142
National Park Service, 75–76
Native Americans, 34, 42, 185
Naturalization Service, 117
NEA (National Education Association), 42–43, 77
New Mexico, 47, 110, 141, 157, 193, 198–99
New York Times, 201
Ngo Dinh Diem, 47
Noonan, Peggy, 23
North American Free Trade Agreement (NAFTA), 143
Nunez, Lilly, 32

O'Connor, Sandra Day, 170
Ohio Civil Rights Commission, 27
Operation Bootheel, 110
Operation Linebacker, 134
Orderly Immigration Act, 132
Organ Pipe Cactus National Monument, 174

Paredes, Miguel Ángel, 144
Patriot Act, 92
Pels, Beowulf, 78
Peninsular and Oriental Steam Navigation Company of London, 140
Perdicaris, Ion, 192–93
Perry, Rick, 198
Pittsburgh Tribune-Review, 75
Pope Benedict XVI, 68
posse comitatus, 110
Putin, Vladimir, 92–93

Raisuli, Ahmad Ibn Muhammad, 193
Rand Corporation, 86
Ratzinger, Cardinal Joseph, 68
Reagan, Ronald, 143, 196
Real Guest Act (H.R.3333), 130
Reforma, 56
Regan, Tom, 191
Reid, Richard, 112
Renshon, Stanley A., 202–3
Richardson, Bill, 198–99
Rio Grande, 80, 85, 147–49
Roosevelt, Theodore, 46, 192–93, 195
Rose, Rhonda, 103–6
Rove, Karl, 11
Rumsfeld, Donald, 125
Russian Duma, 95

S.1033/H.R.2330 (Secure America and Orderly Immigration Act), 132
S.1592 (Emergency Medical Treatment and Active Labor Act-EMTALA), 164–65
SALUTE card, 147
Salvatrucha, Mara, 81
Satari, Suliman, 71

SCAAP (State Criminal Alien Assistance Program), 158
Schlessinger, Arthur M., Jr., 29
Schwarzenegger, Arnold, 198
Secure America and Orderly Immigration Act (S.1033/H.R.2330), 132
Sensenbrenner, James, 114, 134
Sierra Club, 174
Silverio, Cristobal, 168
Social Security, 31, 62, 104–5, 128, 188
Sondoval-Marin, Rosalina, 201
Spencer, Robert, 78
State Criminal Alien Assistance Program (SCAAP), 158
Steele, James B., 111, 173
Sun Tzu, 65, 76

TECS (Treasury Enforcement Communications System), 123
terrorists and terrorism, 24, 33, 43–44, 65, 67–69, 71–73, 75, 77–82, 84, 86–87, 89–98, 101–2, 118, 122–23, 125, 129, 137–39, 140–42, 144, 146, 150, 169, 185–87, 192, 195, 202–4
Texas Border Regulators, 134
Texas Border Sheriff's Coalition, 148
Texas National Guard, 198
Tijuana, Mexico, 148–149
Tohono O'odham Indian Reservation (AZ), 83–84
Treasury Enforcement Communications System (TECS), 123
Tucson, AZ, 101, 174

U.S. Census Bureau, 101, 156, 175
U.S. Conference of Catholic Bishops (USCCB), 132
Ullum, Tom, 27
Urrutia, Ryan, 134
USCCB (U.S. Conference of Catholic Bishops), 132

Vance, Larry, 178
Vance, Toni, 177–78
Vassilaros, DiMitri, 75
Villa, Pancho, 193
Vinyard, JoEllen, 49

Wall Street Journal, 111–13
Wal-Mart, 119, 173
Washington, George, 46
Washington Times, 141
Webb, Wellington, 53
Weinberger, Caspar, 143
West, Arvin, 133–34, 148
Western civilization, 24–25, 37–39, 45, 50, 51–52, 65, 68, 70–71, 73, 76–77, 184, 206
Western Union, 11
Williams, Paul, 67
Wilson, Woodrow, 37, 193
Workers World Party, 15

Y-12 National Security Complex, Los Alamos, NM, 138
Yessoufou, Abdoul Masmoud, 142

Zapata County, TX, 84
Zedong, Mao, 47
Zetas, 80–81, 85
Zieve, Sher, 75